Dramatic FAUX FINISHES

Dramatic FAUX FINISHES

Louise Hennigs
Marina Niven

PHOTOGRAPHY
WARREN HEATH
DEIDI VON SCHAEWEN

CREATIVE PUBLISHING international
CHANHASSEN, MINNESOTA

First published in the USA in 2003 by
Creative Publishing international, Inc.

Creative Publishing international, Inc.
18705 Lake Drive East
Chanhassen, Minnesota 55317
1-800-328-3895
www.creativepub.com

President/CEO: Michael Eleftheriou
Vice President/Publisher: Linda Ball
Vice President/Retail Sales: Kevin Haas

ISBN 1-58923-107-4

First published in 2003 by
New Holland Publishers
London • Cape Town • Sydney • Auckland

Publishing manager: Claudia dos Santos
Managing editor: Simon Pooley
Managing art editor: Richard MacArthur
Editor: Gill Gordon
Designer: Petal Palmer
Stylist: Sonya Nel
Production: Myrna Collins
Proofreader: Katja Splettstoesser

Reproduction by Hirt & Carter (Pty) Ltd, Cape Town
Printed and bound in Singapore by Tien Wah Press (Pte) Ltd
10 9 8 7 6 5 4 3 2 1

CONTENTS

ACKNOWLEDGEMENTS

Our special thanks go to Nella Opperman and Charlie Wright for their continuous support, inspiration and teaching; to Tracey Lynch, Mfundo Olifant and Steven Ntshontsho who helped us during the writing and photography; to Warren Heath for taking such beautiful photographs and to his crew, Anthony Debbo and Greg Cox, for endless help, coffee and humor!

INTRODUCTION

Our third book explores different paint techniques for different surfaces. Like any recipe, paint techniques differ enormously according to the 'cook'. There are many variations that are possible—in fact, every book you read will be different.

The techniques illustrated are tried and trusted, as well as tested by trial and error. As we planned the projects and the step-by-step instructions, we made sure they would be successful and easy to follow, since most decorative paint techniques are done by craftsmen and women, not necessarily by professional artists. However, it is interesting to see that as decorative paint techniques become more advanced, artists tend to use them more frequently. Professional artists are often commissioned to execute elaborate murals, while decorative techniques like gilding are used by some artists in their paintings.

As you master the basic techniques, you can experiment endlessly with colors and various ways of achieving different results. The use of scumble glaze with paint means that very little base color is needed to achieve the final result and wonderful transparent luminous effects can be achieved. It is exciting to experiment with paint techniques and it is also therapeutic and fun. The joy of paint is that it can easily be wiped out and you can start again. What a pleasure!

LOUISE HENNIGS & MARINA NIVEN

COLOR

Color is one of the most important aspects to consider when decorating a room. Color choice is very subjective and the final decision could depend on several factors. Consider the function of the room and the atmosphere you want to create. A child's playroom, for example, should be bright, using a range of colors that inspires play and fun, whereas a study should be more subdued, inducing a mood of calm relaxation.

BASIC COLOR THEORY

The primary colors (red, blue and yellow) are hues, the term used to distinguish one color from another. 'Primary' means they cannot be created by mixing, although they can be mixed to create secondary colors (purple, green and orange). These are the basic hues of a standard color wheel.

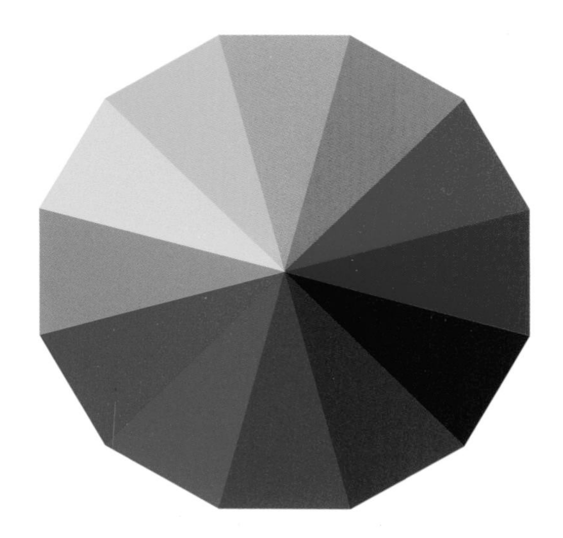

The color wheel
Each primary color lies opposite a secondary color on the color wheel (red opposite green, yellow opposite purple, blue opposite orange). These are called *complementary colors*, because when they are placed next to each other they complement each other by standing out and appearing brighter. For example, a decorator may decide to introduce green accents to complement a predominantly pink area. When complementary colors are mixed together as paint, however, they become muddy gray, effectively neutralizing each other.

Tertiary colors are a mix of primary and secondary colors. For example, purple mixed with red results in a reddish purple, while blue mixed with green gives a bluish green. Tertiary colors have altered in hue but they are still pure in their depth and color.

Tints, tones, values and shades
By adding black or white to any color on the color wheel, a new range of exciting colors emerges. When white is added to a color or hue, that color becomes paler and lighter and is called a *tint*. For example, white added to red creates pink. Depending on how much white is added, the pink will have a pale or deep tonal *value*.

Tone is often used in the same context as *value* and refers to the depth or intensity of a particular color.

When black is added to a color it becomes darker and is called a *shade*. The color will vary in value depending on how much black is added.

Colors are categorized into *warm* and *cool*. Warm colors usually refer to reds, oranges, yellows and any colors that contain them. However, cool colors can overlap, as seen in the tertiary colors on the color wheel. It is possible to have warm yellow-greens or cool purple-reds.

Earthy tones
Yellow ochre, raw and burnt sienna, raw and burnt umber, Indian red, Venetian red and chrome oxide green are all found in clay or stone.

When ground to a fine powder, these colors can be mixed with a binder to make natural pigments. The first artists, who made their marks in the form of rock paintings, mixed pigments with animal fat, blood, milk or plant sap to create usable mixtures. Natural chalk was used for white and carbon, from charcoal, for black.

COLOR MIXING
With the development of synthetic pigments, virtually any hue, tint, shade or variation thereof is commercially available in a number of different mediums. A full range of colors in artists' or students' oils, artists' and students' acrylics, gouache and watercolors can be bought at art stores.

It is important to experiment if you want to create your own colors, but don't be alarmed if you find that your mixture does not produce the color you thought it would. In theory, two primary colors can be mixed to create a secondary color, but in practice, the result is often duller than expected.

To mix a pale color or tint, start with a white base and add small quantities of the pure color until it is as pale as you want it to be. Due to their pigment composition, some colors are stronger than others. If you start with a pure color you could end up using a lot of white to get it pale enough, and waste a lot of paint.

Black is not always the best option to darken other colors, as it can often change them completely or make them appear dull.

For example, adding black to yellow turns it olive green. Instead, use raw or burnt umber, or even a darker hue of yellow. Yellow ochre or raw sienna will produce a darker shade that is rich and lively.

If a color is too bright or crisp in its natural state, add a few drops of its complementary color to obtain a slight dulling without making the color muddy. Complementary colors can also be used to cool a warm color or add warmth to a cool color.

Pastel colors premixed by a paint supplier tend to be very 'sweet' and ice-cream-like. Adding a few drops of raw umber or the complementary color will reduce the glare without changing the overall effect.

When mixing either water- or oil-based paints, always use a brilliant white base to mix pastel colors and a transparent base to mix dark colors.

The color swatches shown below are the basic paint colors used throughout this book. The swatches on the following pages show how to obtain the colors used in some of the projects. Practice mixing the correct colors before you begin working.

Commercially mixed colors

Most paint manufacturers produce, or can blend, a vast spectrum of colors. Coded paint swatches are available as a fan deck or individual swatches to use for matching fabrics or colors.

When you have reached a decision about the color, a paint supplier will mix up any color needed in the type of paint most suitable for the project.

Start off with the smallest amount of paint that the store is prepared to mix, usually one quart (one liter). Paint a test patch on a sample board or directly onto the wall. (Make a sample board from a smooth piece of hard-board or masonite that is primed and undercoated with the same products used on the walls.) Often, the color will dry differently to the swatch, depending on the type of paint or the wall's surface. Use a sample board to check whether the color will work in different lighting, such as daylight, artificial light at night, or in shadow. You can also use the sample board to test decorative techniques. Once you are satisfied with the color and the technique, buy the amount of paint you require to complete the project.

BROWN LEATHER

Base color: honey beige

Burnt sienna

Burnt umber

Raw umber

GREEN LEATHER (VARIATION)

Base color: hookers green

Burnt umber with hookers green

Black

Raw umber

RED LEATHER (VARIATION)

Base color: alizarin crimson

Alizarin crimson with raw sienna

Alizarin crimson with burnt sienna

Raw umber

SHADING ON A BALUSTRADE

Darkest shadows: black with raw umber and a little white

To obtain in-between shades, add a little white

Add more white to get a dark gray shade

Palest gray, almost a white glaze, for highlights

CLOUDS IN A BLUE SKY

Ultramarine or cobalt blue and white for the sky

Ultramarine with a little raw sienna and white for dark clouds

Add alizarin crimson and white to cloud mix for mid-tones

White with a little ultramarine and raw sienna for highlights

GRISAILLE

Base color: gray and white

Shadow: raw umber and white with gray

Shadow: darker raw umber with gray and black

Darkest shadow: add more black to the mixture

Light shadows: add white to the mixture

Base color: mid-tone gray

White for final highlights

NATURAL PINE

Base color and first glaze: raw sienna, yellow ochre and white

Lighter knots: burnt umber with raw sienna

Detail within the knots: add a little black to burnt umber

Darker knots: burnt umber

MAHOGANY

Base color:
terracotta red

First working:
burnt umber

Second working:
burnt sienna and
raw umber

Add more burnt
sienna for a redder
mahogany

LIGHT OAK

Base color:
rich golden corn
(raw sienna and
white)

Raw umber with
raw sienna

Check roller:
burnt umber and
raw umber

TRAVERTINE

Base color:
sandy beige

Yellow ochre and
white

Raw sienna and
white

Raw umber and
white

Burnt sienna,
raw umber and
white

EGYPTIAN GREEN MARBLE

Base color:
black

Terre-verte
(green earth)

Terre-verte and a
little white

Terre-verte and a
little more white

Pale terre-verte

SIENA MARBLE

Raw sienna

Burnt sienna

Raw umber

Burnt umber

USING DIFFERENT COLORANTS

COLORANT	STEP ONE	STEP TWO	STEP THREE
Universal stainers: Can be used to color oil- or water-based paints.	Add a few drops of the appropriate colored stainer to a container of paint. Remember, mix pale colors into a white base and mix dark colors into a transparent base.	Stir the paint well. Paint a test patch on a piece of card and dry it with a hair dryer. Oil-based paint will take longer to dry than water-based and you will notice that the wet color differs from the dry paint color.	Continue adding small amounts of stainer to the paint, testing it each time until you have achieved the desired color.
Artists' oils: Can only be mixed with oil-based paint, glaze or varnish. They give the purest color and are best used for intricate decorative finishes such as stone, faux marble and wood graining.	Squeeze about 1¼" (30 mm) of a single color or a combination of colors onto a palette. Using a palette knife, mix them together until the desired color is achieved.	Scrape the color mixture into a small bowl or jar and add enough mineral spirits to dilute it to the consistency of thin cream. Stir to remove all the lumps.	Slowly add a few drops of this mixture at a time to a paint, glaze or varnish until the desired color is achieved. A few drops of terebine driers can be added to speed up the drying process.
Artists' acrylics: Can only be mixed with water-based paint, glaze or varnish. Some acrylic colors are more opaque than others and can result in a cloudy effect when used to stain transparent glaze or varnish.	Squeeze about 1¼" (30 mm) of a single color or a combination of colors onto a palette. Using a palette knife, mix them together until the desired color is achieved.	Scrape the color mixture into a small bowl or jar and add enough water to dilute it to the consistency of thin cream. Stir to remove all the lumps.	Slowly add a few drops of this mixture at a time to a paint, glaze or varnish until the desired color is achieved.

MATERIALS & EQUIPMENT

Paints, glazes, varnishes and brushes are among the materials and equipment needed for the decorative paint finishes described in this book. Most of the items can be found at your local paint dealer or art store, although some of the finishing brushes and tools may have to be purchased from stores specializing in decorative paint supplies.

PAINTS, GLAZES & VARNISHES

When choosing materials and equipment, use the best products you can afford. The better the tools, the easier it will be to master the technique.

Paint manufacturers produce so many different types of paint that choosing the right one for a particular task can be daunting when confronted with the variety available. It helps, therefore, to have a basic understanding of paint, its composition, uses and applications before beginning a project.

All paints are made up of pigment, which provides the color; a binder or medium in which the pigment is suspended and which binds the paint to a surface; and a solvent, which dilutes the mixture to make it flow smoothly and evenly. The solvent evaporates in the drying process and leaves an even, dry coating on the surface. The durability, hardness and absorbency of a painted surface depends on the type of pigment, binder and solvent used.

TYPES OF PAINT

Paint manufacturers produce two types of paint: contractors' quality and a superior version. The difference is in the price and the paint's durability, with contractors' paint being much cheaper. Some less-expensive water-based paints are dry, dull and chalky, and often too absorbent for decorative paint finishes, yet some contractors' paints are of such superior quality that they dry as strong as any oil-based paint and can be used as a base coat for oil-based decorative finishes.

Storing paint

When you finish painting, ensure that the can's rim and lid are both free of paint. Press the lid down firmly and give it a few knocks with a rubber

RECIPES FOR MIXING GLAZES

WATER-BASED GLAZE

Mix the following parts by volume:

1 part water-based wall paint

2 parts water-based scumble glaze

1 part water

This is an approximate mixture. The consistency of the glaze may need to vary according to the paint finishing technique selected.

Some techniques require a diluted or thin glaze, so add more water; others need transparency, so add more glaze. In humid climates, add extra paint to assist in the drying process. The color comes from the premixed wall paint but it can be altered by adding universal stainers or artists' acrylic paint.

OIL-BASED GLAZE

Mix the following parts by volume:

1 part oil-based wall paint

1 part oil-based scumble glaze

1 part mineral spirits

This is an approximate mixture. The consistency of the glaze may need to vary according to the paint finishing technique selected.

Some techniques require a diluted or thin glaze, needing more mineral spirits to be added, while others need transparency, so add more glaze to the mixture.

The color comes from the premixed wall paint but it can be altered by adding universal stainers or artists' oil paint.

mallet or your heel to secure it. This will keep air out and stop a skin from forming on the surface of the paint. If a skin does form, remove it and strain the remaining paint through a stocking to remove any lumps.

Store paint, glaze, varnish and solvents away from direct heat or sunlight. Make sure all containers are labeled with their contents and where they were used, so that you can find them without opening the containers.

Strong-colored glazes

Some finishes need a very pure, intense-colored glaze (for example, faux leather or fantasy marble finishes). These strong colors can be achieved by using artists' oil paints instead of oil-based wall paint. Because of the intensity of a strong-colored glaze, it is not necessary to make huge quantities of it at a time.

To make about half a cup of glaze, squeeze approximately 2" (50 mm) of artists' oil paint in a single color, or combine the colors you need to make up the same quantity. Add a teaspoon of mineral spirits and blend the paint to make a thick paste, adding more solvent if required. Add equal quantities of scumble glaze and mineral spirits to this paste, one tablespoon at a time. Test as you mix to see if the glaze requires more glaze than solvent or vice versa, depending on the required consistency.

Antiquing glaze

Follow the instructions for strong-colored glazes at left, using raw umber artists' oil paint. This will give a basic antiquing glaze which can be made stronger by adding more color, or weaker by adding more glaze. Adding more solvent will 'water' down the consistency.

You can also adjust the color. For example, for an aluminum leaf finish, the antiquing glaze is made with Payne's gray, ivory and black artists' oils, while burnt umber can be used for a warmer antique color.

Testing the base coat

If you are applying a paint finish to an already painted surface and you are not sure if the base is an oil- or water-based paint, there is a very easy way of finding out. Take a piece of cotton wool or a soft cloth, wet it with denatured alcohol/methylated spirits and rub a small area with it. If the paint dissolves and comes off on the cloth, then the wall has been painted with water-based paint. If the cloth is clean, it is an oil-based surface.

Drying times for paint

Paint drying times vary considerably from one type of paint to another. In general, water-based paint dries faster than oil-based paint.

When painting the preparation coats, refer to the instructions and drying time on the paint can. However, it is best to allow 12 to 24 hours between each layer of primer, undercoat and top coat.

All paint reaches a surface dryness sooner than the drying time indicated. In other words, it will feel dry to the touch, but below the surface it will still need time to set and dry fully before the next layer can be applied.

The drying time of a glaze will determine how much time can be spent working on a decorative finish. Retarders or driers can be added to either prolong or speed up the drying time, but this will depend on the type of glaze and the technique being used. Always allow a glaze to dry thoroughly (12 to 24 hours) before applying the next layer of glaze or varnish.

Paint quantities

Estimating how much paint is required for a specific job is always a challenge. It depends on how many coats are required, how absorbent the surface is and the degree to which the paint will be diluted. Here is a rough but fairly accurate guide to buying paint.

When applying a full-strength base coat, one quart (one liter) of paint will cover approximately 24 sq ft (8 sq m) of wall. A wash or glaze will use less paint as it is diluted, therefore one quart (one liter) of glaze will cover approximately 60 sq ft (20 sq m).

Measure the walls and ceiling in square feet or square meters to calculate how much paint is required.

WATER-BASED PRODUCTS

TYPE OF PAINT	COMPOSITION	SOLVENT AND CLEANER
Water-based wall paint Also known as latex vinyl emulsion or PVA (polyvinyl acrylic). Available in flat/matte, satin/midsheen/eggshell and high gloss finishes.	Pigment: synthetic or natural color powder. Binder: acrylic resin. Solvent: water.	Water: to dilute the paint and wash the brushes.
Artists' acrylic paints Available in tubes or tubs.	Concentrated pigments in water-soluble base.	Water: to dilute the paint and wash the brushes.
Acrylic scumble glaze (Also known as acrylic medium).	Acrylic resin suspended in water with a retardant added to slow the drying process. Appears milky when wet but dries clear.	Water: to dilute the paint and wash the brushes.
Water-based varnish Available in flat/matte, gloss and suede/midsheen.	Tough acrylic resin suspended in water. Appears milky when wet but dries clear.	Water: to dilute the paint and wash the brushes.

WATER-BASED PRODUCTS

USES	CAN BE MIXED WITH	PROS AND CONS
For general exterior and interior paint work on walls and ceilings. Used as a base coat for water-based decorative finishes.	Acrylic scumble glaze and water to make a glaze for decorative finishes.	**+ Factor:** Dries quickly and is waterproof when dry. Cleans with water . **- Factor:** Dark colors lack depth. Needs protection in high-traffic areas.
For small-scale decorative painting such as furniture or detail on murals. Can also be used for stencilling.	Water to dilute it and make a wash, or can be added to acrylic scumble glaze and paint as a colorant.	**+ Factor:** Waterproof when dry, strong durable colors. **- Factor:** Expensive when used as a colorant. Quick-drying, so requires an experienced painter.
To facilitate decorative effects by creating a glaze that is transparent and has a longer drying time than paint. Can be used for most decorative paint effects.	Water-based wall paint and water, tinted with universal stainers or artists' acrylic paint to make a glaze.	**+ Factor:** Odorless, less toxic than oil-based glaze, quick drying. **- Factor:** Colors not as brilliant as oil-based glaze. Quick drying, so skill and speed are required when working.
To protect all water-based paint finishes.	Can be tinted with universal stainers if required.	**+ Factor:** Odorless, quick-drying, does not discolor. **- Factor:** If applied too thickly, it will dry cloudy.

OIL-BASED PRODUCTS

TYPE OF PAINT	COMPOSITION	SOLVENT AND CLEANER
Oil-based wall paint Also known as alkyd, enamel. Available in flat/matte, gloss and satin/midsheen/eggshell. Some manufacturers produce a non-drip paint that is thixotropic (gel-based).	Pigment: synthetic color. Binder: alkyd or synthetic resin, drying oil. Solvent: Mineral spirits.	Mineral spirits to dilute and wash brushes.
Artists' oil paints Available in tubes. Student quality is less expensive but colors are not as saturated as artists' quality.	Finely ground pigments mixed with linseed oil and drying oils.	Mineral spirits to dilute and wash brushes.
Oil-based scumble glaze This has a creamy color and thick consistency. It dries clear and transparent but cannot be used as a paint on its own as it will not dry.	Whiting/chalk, linseed oil, mineral spirits.	Mineral spirits to dilute and wash brushes.
Oil-based varnish Also called polyurethane varnish. Available in flat/matte, gloss and suede/midsheen.	Synthetic oils and resins.	Mineral spirits to dilute and wash brushes.

OIL-BASED PRODUCTS

USES	CAN BE MIXED WITH	PROS AND CONS
Interior walls in high traffic areas. Excellent for protecting interior and exterior woodwork. Used as a base for oil-based decorative finishes.	Oil-based scumble glaze, diluted with mineral spirits to make a glaze for decorative finishes.	**+ Factor:** Strong and durable. Water resistant. Has a good depth of color. **- Factor:** Slow-drying (6–12 hours). Fumes are unpleasant and dangerous in unventilated areas.
Primarily for painting on canvas, but in decorative finishes it provides strong colors to tint glazes.	Mineral spirits to dilute. Add to oil-based scumble glaze and paint as a colorant.	**+ Factor:** Strong colors even when diluted. Slow drying allows for longer working time. **- Factor:** Expensive if used in large quantities.
To facilitate decorative effects by creating a glaze that is transparent and has a longer drying time than paint. Can be used for most decorative effects.	Oil-based wall paint or mineral spirits tinted with universal stainers or artists' oil paint to make a glaze.	**+ Factor:** Extends color well. Slow drying allows for longer working time. **- Factor:** Can turn yellow when exposed to direct sun for any length of time.
To protect all oil-based painted surfaces and raw or stained wood.	Can be tinted with artists' oils if required.	**+ Factor:** Durable, with a strong, protective coat. **- Factor:** Can turn yellow with time.

BRUSHES & SPECIALTY EQUIPMENT

Brushes are manufactured in a wide range of sizes and shapes and come in different qualities, each of which has a specific use. The most commonly found brushes are those used for household painting and varnishing. Specialty artists' brushes are more purpose-specific and can be used for either oil, acrylic or water-color painting.

Standard flat decorators' brushes
Sizes vary from ½" to 6" (12 to 150 mm). Flat brushes are used for painting walls or furniture.

Japanese hake
Used for softening and blending colors.

Badger softener
Used to soften and blend marks in oil-based and water-based glazes.

Hog softener
Used as a stippling brush to disperse glaze evenly over the surface and eliminate brush strokes. Hog hair is firm but flexible.

Flogger
Creates a broken texture, resembling wood grain, when flicked against wet glaze. Horsehair filaments make it very flexible. (Can also be used for dragging.)

Specialty brushes for decorative paint finishes can be obtained from local paint dealers or art stores. All brushes are similarly constructed, although their shape, size and type of bristle may vary. The bristle, or filament, is fixed into the ferrule (the metal piece holding the filament) with epoxy resin and the handle is attached with rivets or nails. Where the filaments enter the ferrule, fillers separate them, allowing the brush to hold more paint.

Brushes are made with natural filaments (animal hair or bristle), or synthetic filaments (nylon or polyester). Natural filaments are more durable and give a better finish, but are more expensive than synthetic filaments.

Flat nylon brushes
Used for a variety of oil- or acrylic-based finishes.

Artists' fitches (left and right).
Can be flat, round or filbert (pointed), and made from natural or synthetic materials. Used for all fine decorative work in oils and acrylics.

Rubber rocker (left and right). Used to create the heart grain in wood finishes.

Check roller
Used to create the lighter 'flecks' that are the characteristic markings in oak grain.

Overgrainer
Used to create the parallel lines of wood grain. (Also called a bristle pencil.)

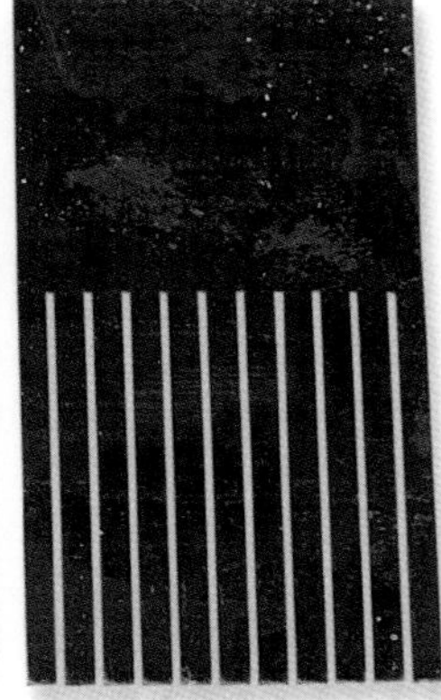

Metal graining combs
Steel combs are used to create the fine scratch lines that occur in some wood grains.

Foam applicator
Used for applying glue in decoupage.

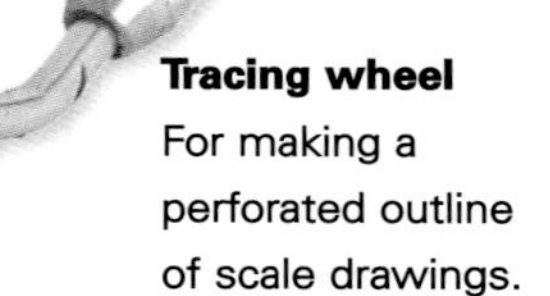

Tracing wheel
For making a perforated outline of scale drawings.

BRUSH CARE

To buy all the brushes required for the finishes described in this book will be costly, so it pays to treat them well and clean them thoroughly each time they are used. If your budget allows, buy two sets of decorators' brushes; one set for white paint only and the other for use with colored paints.

Some brushes are specifically made for water-based paints and others for oil-based paints. Try to keep each type separate because 'water-based' brushes are often made with nylon filaments and will last longer if they are only washed in water.

The first step in brush care is learning to use the brush correctly.

When loading the paintbrush (dipping it into paint), do not submerge the filaments more than halfway. If paint gets into the filaments where they are attached to the ferrule, the brush will be difficult to clean and its life span will be shortened.

Never stir paint with a brush that you are going to use for painting. Always use a stirring stick, wooden spoon or a palette knife.

As you work, you may find that paint starts clogging and drying at the top of the filaments, especially if you work on a large area. This cannot be helped, as with each brush stroke, the paint will automatically work its way up. This is why it is advisable to have two identical brushes. When the first brush starts clogging with paint, suspend it in the appropriate solvent to clean it, and continue working on the project using the other brush.

Most paint brushes have a hole at the end of the handle. If not, make a hole big enough to take a length of thin wire. When cleaning the brush, suspend the filaments in the solvent, but do not allow the filaments to rest on the bottom of the container as this will cause them to lose their shape.

If you need to take a break from painting, or are waiting for one color to dry before you can continue, either suspend the brush in solvent for a brief period or wrap it in plastic wrap to prevent it from drying out. Leaving brushes hanging in mineral spirits will cause the filaments to deteriorate.

WASHING BRUSHES

Always wash brushes well at the end of each painting session, using the appropriate solvent: wash brushes used for water-based paint with water, and those used for oil-based paint with mineral spirits.

Prepare two containers of solvent, the first one to get the initial bulk of the paint out of the filaments and the other for a second wash, to ensure that all the paint is removed. Squeeze out excess solvent and dry the brush with a cloth or paper towel before washing it again in clean solvent.

If a stubborn residue of paint remains near the ferrule, take a wire brush and work it through the filaments, working away from the ferrule. If you are using water-based paint, soak the brush in denatured alcohol/methylated spirits to dislodge the residue.

When all the paint has been washed out in the solvent, wash the brush with mild dishwashing liquid and cold water. Rinse well.

Get rid of excess water by rolling the brush handle between the palms of your hands, spinning the water out of the filaments. Reshape the bristles and hang the brush on a wire hook to dry before packing it away.

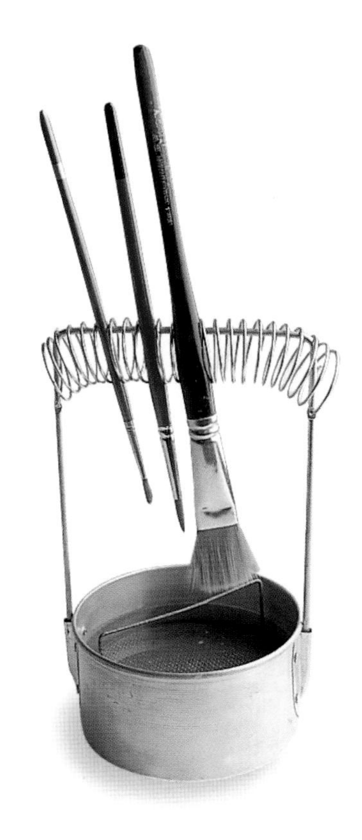

Suspend brushes after washing.

CARING FOR ARTISTS' AND SPECIALTY BRUSHES

Diligent care will lengthen the life of specialty brushes considerably. Never leave them standing in the cleaning solvent as this will bend the filaments, damage their structure and make painting difficult. If you are waiting for one layer to dry before you can continue, rinse the brushes in the appropriate solvent and wrap them in plastic to prevent them from drying out. If you leave them for longer than a few hours, you must clean them properly. If you want specialty brushes to maintain their softness and flexibility, and last a long time, treat them as you would your own hair.

To remove paint, use your fingers to work the appropriate solvent through the filaments, then rinse the brush thoroughly in clean solvent. Wipe off any excess on paper towels, then wash the brush with shampoo and conditioner. When the brush is thoroughly clean and rinsed, wipe off excess water and dry with a hair dryer.

STORING BRUSHES

Some brushes come with a protective cardboard sleeve and, once they are dry, it is advisable to keep them in this sleeve, or wrapped in tissue paper or a soft cloth, as this will help to maintain the shape of the filaments, thereby prolonging the life of the brush.

Specialty brushes

When dry, wrap the brushes in tissue paper or a soft cloth, taking care not to crush the filaments. Store them in a box or on a shelf where they can lie flat without any risk of being damaged.

Artists' brushes

Take a drop of liquid soap between your thumb and forefinger and coat the filaments with a thin layer of soap, making sure they come together in a neat point; the soap will dry and this will protect the filaments.

Stand the brushes, filaments up, in a jar or keep them in a cloth pouch or wrapped in tissue paper. Remember to wash off the soap before using the brush again.

SURFACE PREPARATION

Preparing your working surface is a time-consuming yet important part of painting. A newly prepared surface provides a base for paints and glazes and any defects will show through in the final finish. The basic principles of clean, sound and smooth should apply to all surfaces, but the amount and type of preparation required will depend on the original state. Once you have decided on a decorative finish, ensure that the object or area to be painted is suitable for that technique.

SURFACE PREPARATION

TYPE OF SURFACE	CLEANING	FILLING
Painted walls in good condition	Wash with a solution of TSP (trisodium phosphate) and warm water (see p126). Rinse with clean water; dry.	Remove any picture hooks and fill the holes with an all-purpose filling agent.
Painted walls in bad condition	Scrape off any loose and peeling paint but avoid removing plaster.	Enlarge any cracks by running the point of a scraper through them. Dust out the cracks and fill with all-purpose wall filler. If the cracks are large and deep, fill them in stages, allowing the filler to dry and shrink into the crack.
Walls previously painted in oil-based paint	1. These walls will have to be sanded before washing (see sanding section first). 2. Wash with a solution of TSP and warm water. Rinse off with clean water and allow to dry.	
New walls It is extremely important to leave newly plastered walls to dry out completely before beginning to paint, as this allows salts and chemicals in the plaster to work their way to the surface.	Dust lightly with a brush or cloth. You could also use the brush attachment on a vacuum cleaner.	
Walls previously painted with limewash If these walls are now to be painted in a modern latex or oil-based paint, make sure there is no dampness in the walls as this will result in blistering and peeling later.	Brush the wall with a stiff brush to remove any dust or loose dirt.	

SURFACE PREPARATION

SANDING	PRIMING/UNDERCOATING	BASE COAT
When filler is dry, sand the filled areas until they are smooth.	Prime with undercoat and allow to dry.	Spot-paint with original wall paint.
When dry, sand the filled areas until smooth. Sand the edges of the peeled paint so that they are not noticeable.	Apply universal undercoat to the newly filled cracks and peeled areas.	Paint one coat of base coat in the desired color. Allow 24 hours' drying time before beginning any decorative finish.
Wrap sandpaper over a block of wood and lightly sand over the whole wall. This will key (roughen) the surface so that it will hold new layers of paint. (See cleaning section next.)		Apply two coats of the appropriate oil- or water-based paint. Allow 24 hours' drying time between each coat and before beginning any decorative finish.
	Apply suitable plaster primer or sealer. Ask your local paint dealer to recommend appropriate products, as these differ among manufacturers. Allow primer to dry, then apply a coat of universal undercoat. Allow to dry.	Apply two coats of the appropriate oil- or water-based paint. Allow 24 hours' drying time between each coat and before beginning any decorative finish.
	Apply a coat of bonding liquid followed by a coat of plaster primer or sealer.	Apply two coats of the appropriate oil- or water-based paint. Allow 24 hours' drying time between each coat and before beginning any decorative finish.

SURFACE PREPARATION

TYPE OF SURFACE	CLEANING	FILLING
Concrete floors	Scrub with a wire brush to remove loose paint. Use a suitable solvent to remove glue residue left behind after lifting old tiles. Wash with TSP and water, rinse well and allow to dry.	Filling holes or smoothing surfaces in concrete is time consuming. Use all-purpose exterior or interior filler for small areas. If a floor is badly pitted it is better to reskim with new cement.
Raw wood (new unpainted wood)	Dust with a brush or cloth.	Fill any holes or cracks with wood filler. (This is usually made in different colors, so choose the right one for your type of wood.)
Prepainted woodwork in good condition This also applies to wood that has been stained and varnished.	Wash with TSP to remove any grease, rinse with clean water and allow to dry.	Fill any small nail holes or cracks with commercial wood filler. Use a spackle tool to smooth it off.
Prepainted woodwork in poor condition Avoid complete stripping if at all possible, as it is both messy and time consuming.	If stripping is necessary, apply paint stripper following the product instructions. Wash with TSP and rinse well with fresh water. Alternatively, use a scraper to peel away loose paint or varnish.	Fill any small nail holes or cracks with commercial wood filler. Use a spackle tool to smooth it off.
Metal	Rid the surface of any rust or loose paint by rubbing it down with steel wool or sandpaper. Use a cloth to remove the dust.	

SURFACE PREPARATION

SANDING	PRIMING/UNDERCOATING	BASE COAT
	Apply suitable primer or undercoat. (Your local paint supplier will be able to advise on the correct product.)	Apply two coats of the appropriate oil- or water-based paint. Allow 24 hours' drying time between each coat and before beginning any decorative finish.
Sand lightly between applying the wood filler and the undercoat.	Cover each knot in the wood with two coats of stain-blocking primer, to prevent resin from seeping out and staining the painted surface. Apply a coat of pink or white wood primer; dry; apply universal undercoat.	Apply two coats of the appropriate oil- or water-based paint. Allow 24 hours' drying time between each coat and before beginning any decorative finish.
Sand the entire surface regardless of the type of paint to be used. With woodwork, a good key is needed to allow the new layers of paint to adhere well.		Apply two coats of the appropriate oil- or water-based paint. Allow 24 hours' drying time between each coat and before beginning any decorative finish.
Sand the surface with different grades of sandpaper, ending with the finest grade. If large areas of paint remain, sand the edges to make them less visible under the top coat.	Apply two coats of pink or white oil-based wood primer, allowing it to dry well between coats.	Apply two coats of the appropriate oil- or water-based paint. Allow 24 hours' drying time between each coat and before beginning any decorative finish.
	Apply a coat of rust-proof paint followed by a coat of metal primer.	Apply two coats of the appropriate oil- or water-based paint. Allow 24 hours' drying time between each coat and before beginning any decorative finish.

SURFACE PREPARATION

TYPE OF SURFACE	CLEANING	FILLING
Plastic	First wash with denatured alcohol/methylated spirits and then with a strong detergent.	
Ceramic (Usually tiled floors or walls.)	Wipe off all greasy residue with acetone.	

Even a seemingly old or 'distressed' wall requires proper surface preparation if it is to endure.

SURFACE PREPARATION

SANDING	PRIMING/UNDERCOATING	BASE COAT
Roughen the surface with fine sandpaper and then wipe with acetone.	Apply a coat of universal undercoat or plastic primer (if this is available at your local paint shop).	Apply two coats of the appropriate oil- or water-based paint. Allow 24 hours' drying time between coats.
	Some manufacturers produce a ceramic primer. If this is not available from your local paint supplier, use a metal primer to allow the base paint to adhere to the surface.	Apply two coats of the appropriate oil- or water-based paint. Allow 24 hours' drying time between each coat and before beginning any decorative finish.

Proper preparation may be time-consuming, but it is essential if you want to achieve a good paint finish.

DECORATIVE FINISHES

The projects introduced in this section have been chosen because they are all variations on basic paint finishing techniques such as manipulating glazes, or disturbing surfaces with different implements to create a number of exciting decorative and faux effects. Although some of the techniques demonstrated may require a bit more skill than others, they are all very achievable, even for beginners.

MOIRÉ (WATERED TAFFETA EFFECT)

SHOPPING LIST

MATERIALS

Water-based:

Water-based wall paint in the color of your choice for the base coat

White water-based wall paint

Acrylic scumble glaze

Water

Oil-based:

Oil-based wall paint in the color of your choice for the base coat

White oil-based wall paint

Oil-based scumble glaze

Mineral spirits

EQUIPMENT

Brushes:

Roller or decorators' brush for base coat

3" (75 mm) decorators' brush for glaze

Flogger brush

Rubber rocker or heart grainer with fine grain

Rags or paper towel

Protective latex gloves

Plastic or canvas drop cloths to protect surfaces

Moiré, or watermarked fabric, was once used to cover walls or to line the insides of cupboards, giving a very opulent effect. This paint finish is a fun and more economical way of emulating the original silk fabric. To carry out this technique a rubber rocker, or heart graining tool, which is usually used in wood graining techniques, is used. It takes some skill and dexterity to complete a whole wall with a moiré finish, so work on a smaller area first to get acquainted with the technique.

1 Prepare the surface and apply two coats of the chosen base color.

2 Mix a white glaze using equal parts of white wall paint, scumble glaze and solvent.

3 Apply a thin layer of the glaze to the surface using a 3" (75 mm) brush. Work from the top of the wall to the bottom in a strip approximately 12" (30 cm) wide.

4 Wipe the brush clean on a rag and, applying slight pressure, drag the brush through the glaze again, thus removing excess glaze and at the same time creating a dragged grain in the glaze.

5 The rubber rocker, or heart-grainer, has a curved surface with concentric half-circles molded into the rubber or plastic. Hold the rocker with both hands in the middle. Start at the top with the center of the circular grain against the wall and your knuckles angled towards the wall (see pp 80–83).

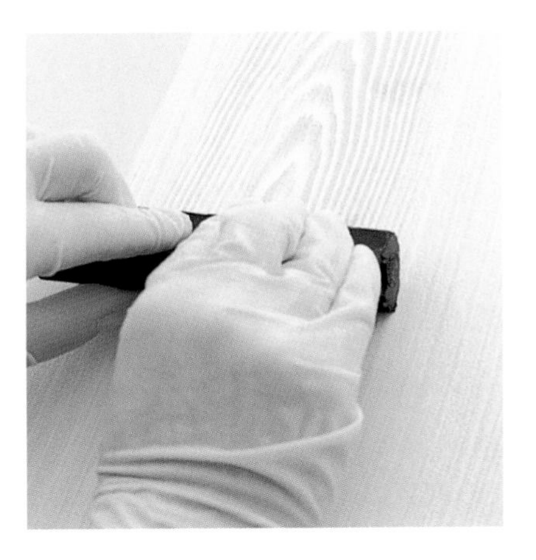

6 Slowly drag the rocker down the wall, rolling it back and forth as you move down, to create the moiré markings in the glaze. Do not stop until you reach the bottom, as this will cause a break in the pattern.

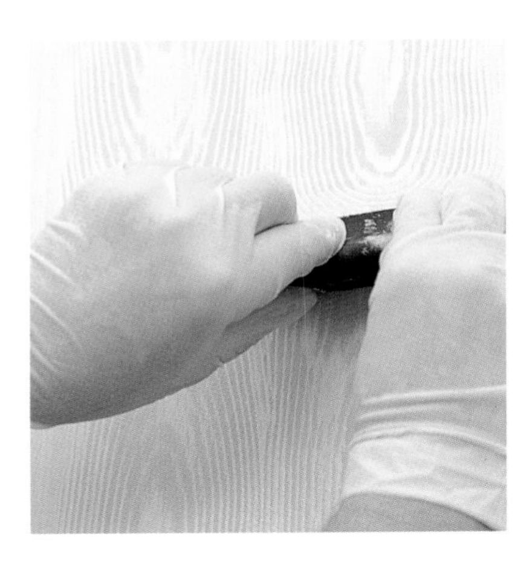

7 Clean the excess glaze from the grooves of the rocker and turn it over so that the outer circles are now against the wall. Place the rocker next to the previous working, slightly overlapping it. Repeat the process.

8 Continue doing a few rows at a time but keep checking the first working. When the glaze has started setting take a flogger brush and very lightly stroke the brush down the moiré pattern. (Remember that water-based glaze sets faster than oil-based glaze).

9 Next, stroke the flogger horizontally across the pattern to create the impression of woven fabric.

Moiré is a luxurious finish.

FAUX LEATHER

SHOPPING LIST

MATERIALS

Light honey-brown oil-based wall paint for the base color
Oil-based scumble glaze
Artists' oils in burnt sienna, burnt umber and raw umber
Mineral spirits
Liquid driers
Oil-based varnish

EQUIPMENT

Brushes:
2" (50 mm) decorators' brush or roller for base coat
Japanese hake or badger softener
Fine sandpaper (220 and 440 grit)
Ruler or measuring tape
Thin card
Paint tray covered by a plastic bag
Containers for mixing paint
Gold trimming tape
Craft knife
T-shirt or other soft fabric for bob
Protective latex gloves
Plastic or canvas drop cloths to protect surfaces

Tip Make a bob from a square of cotton knit fabric filled with cotton wool and secured with a rubber band.

This relatively easy technique is effective on furniture and on wall panelling. It imitates old polished leather and will give a study or office a wonderful atmosphere of warmth and character. It can also be very effective on furniture or boxes, which are often trimmed with gold. A faux leather finish is usually done in traditional leather colors, such as dark shades of brown, burgundy or green (see p12). The base color should be a few shades lighter than natural leather.

1 Prepare the surface well and ensure that it is smooth with no imperfections as this will result in unwanted marks in the finish.
Apply two coats of a light honey-brown base coat, sanding lightly with 220 grit sandpaper between each coat.

When the final coat is dry, lightly sand with 440 grit paper just to key (roughen) the surface, then dust well with a cloth. Avoid touching the object with your hands after this, as the natural oils in your skin will leave marks that could affect the finish.

2 Mix three separate glazes using artists' oils in raw umber, burnt umber and burnt sienna. Follow the glaze recipe on page 18, adding a few drops of liquid driers. The strength of the artists' oils will make the drying time very long. Work in a dust-free area.

3 Apply the glazes in big patches, starting with the darkest color (burnt umber). Use a 2" (50 mm) decorators' brush and leave gaps between the patches. These patches must be done in drifts so that the final result is not a mass of small patches resembling either an animal print or a checkerboard. Fill in the gaps with more big patches of the other two glazes (raw umber and burnt sienna).

4 Make a bob using soft mutton cloth or fine T-shirt material (see tip on opposite page). Lightly butter the bob with the burnt sienna glaze. Buttering the bob stops it from removing the glaze from the object, but overloading the bob will result in extra glaze being added to the surface, which should be avoided.

5 Using the bob, dab over the whole surface to blend the colors and eliminate the brush strokes, creating an even, mottled surface. To lighten an area, wipe the bob to remove excess glaze, then dab the area with the bob to lift the glaze.

6 Barely touching the surface, lightly polish it with a Japanese hake or badger softener.

7 Allow to dry completely. At this stage you can apply an optional gold line to finish off the project (as shown above). This is easily done using gold trim tape which is used in the automotive trade. Decide on the width of your border (the distance from the edge of the object will indicate the position of the gold line). In this demonstration we have placed the trim 2½" (60 mm) from the edge. It is important to bear in mind that the thin glaze layer of the leather finish is very fragile at this point and you must be careful not to damage it.

8 To apply the optional gold trim, cut four long strips of card the length and width of the borders and join them together to make a frame. If you want to make a curved corner, mark and cut out four quarter circles from another piece of card and stick them into the corners of the frame.

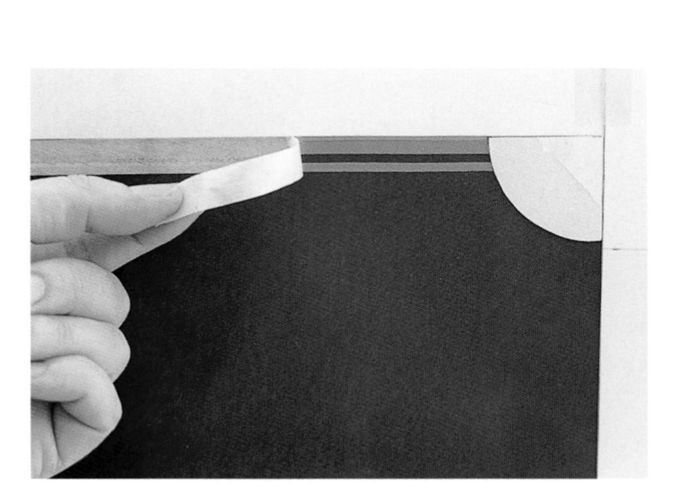

9 Position the frame on the surface and weigh it down. Stick the tape onto the leather finish in line with the edge of the guide. In order to get a round corner, push the tape down and stretch it bit by bit into the curve. Cut away any small overlapping pieces of tape with a craft knife.

10 Varnish with semi-gloss oil-based varnish.

The natural leather of a chair is complemented by the warm tones of a faux leather coffee table.

FAUX IVORY

SHOPPING LIST

MATERIALS

White oil-based wall paint

Artists' oil paint in raw umber

Oil-based scumble glaze

Mineral spirits

Terebine driers

Gloss varnish

EQUIPMENT

Brushes:

2" (50 mm) decorators' brush or small foam roller for base coat

Flat nylon artists' brush

Fine sandpaper (220 grit)

Graph paper

Water-soluble pencil

Ruler

Craft knife

Thin card

Mutton cloth or soft T-shirt fabric

Protective latex gloves

Plastic or canvas drop cloths to protect surfaces

The use of ivory and bone for decorative objects was widely practiced for centuries, but has come to an end in most places due to the ban on the trade in ivory. Nonetheless, these objects remain beautiful and desirable. This easy paint technique can be used to recreate the look of authentic ivory. Small wooden boxes or flat picture frames are ideal for a marquetry pattern in this decorative finish but it can be equally effective as an inlaid design on dark furniture.

1 Prepare the surface and paint with two coats of white oil-based wall paint. The surface must be very smooth for this technique to be convincing, so sand with 220 grit sandpaper between each coat.

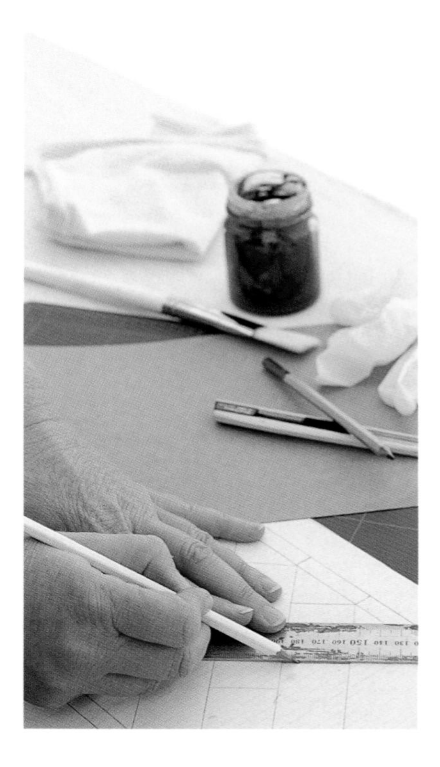

2 Plan the design of the marquetry pattern on graph paper. Measure the box and draw it to scale so that you can design the pattern according to the shape of the box. Keep in mind that the natural size of the tusk would limit the size of the ivory pieces in the design.

3 Transfer your design to the box by measuring it out and drawing it with a water-soluble pencil.

4 Use a craft knife to cut into the wood in straight lines, to represent the edges of each piece of 'ivory'.

5 To make the characteristic distress lines and fine cracks, first decide on the direction of the cracks in each piece. Then, using a piece of card to mask each edge, work away from the card and cut fine lines into the paint surface. Treat each piece of 'ivory' individually and avoid repetition and uniformity in the cut markings. This will give a more authentic rendering.

6 Make an antiquing glaze using the raw umber artists' oil paint and scumble glaze, adding terebine driers (see p19) to help the glaze set faster.

7 Paint the glaze over the whole surface with the flat nylon artists' brush. Work back and forth and in opposite directions to ensure that the glaze penetrates all the cut lines.

8 While the glaze is still wet, use a piece of mutton cloth to wipe just enough glaze off to allow the residue of the pigment to stain the white paint so that it resembles the color of ivory.

9 When completely dry, apply two coats of gloss varnish.

A trinket box has been transformed into an object of subtle beauty.

STRIPES & CHECKS

SHOPPING LIST

MATERIALS

Water-based wall paint

Acrylic scumble glaze

Water

EQUIPMENT

2" (50 mm) decorators' paint brush

Ruler and tape measure

Plumb line and chalk line

Thick card for template

Craft knife

Water-soluble pencil

Plastic putty or low-tack double-sided tape

Protective latex gloves

Plastic or canvas drop cloths to protect surfaces

SURFACE PREPARATION

If necessary, prepare the wall surface and paint with two coats of the desired base color. If the wall is already painted white and is in good condition you can apply the stripes directly in any color you choose. However, you could also have a colored background and paint white stripes. The possibilities are endless.

Stripes and checks can be used very effectively to decorate either an entire room or just individual pieces of furniture. Stripes in any subtle color will give a wall a certain depth and definition. Inspiration for stripes and checks can be found in curtaining or upholstery fabrics, tartans and even tea towels! The success of a stripe or check is in the accuracy of measuring the surface and in placing the design.

STRIPES

1 Decide on the width of the stripes and measure the wall to determine how many stripes will fit along it. In the step-by-step demonstration we have made the stripes 8" (20 cm) wide.

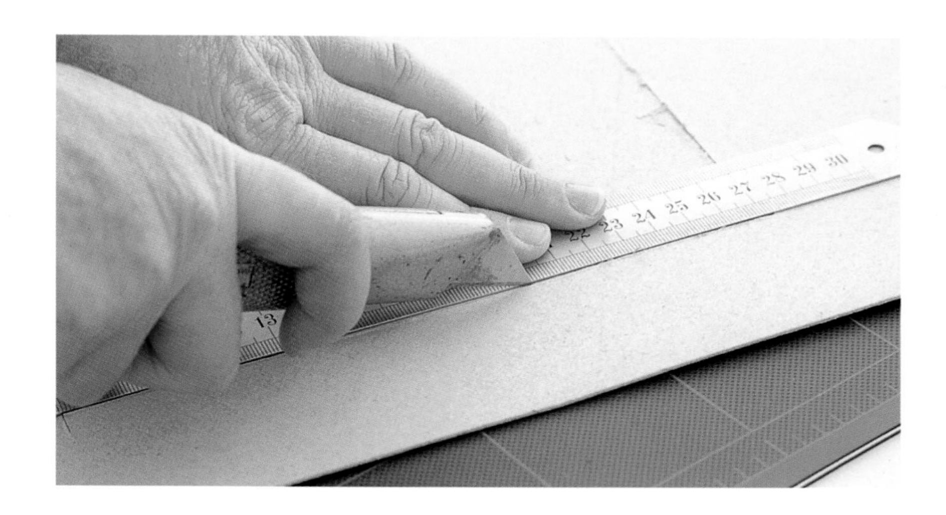

2 To make a template for the stripe, cut a piece of card 16" × 24" (40 × 60 cm). Cut out a rectangular piece from the middle, leaving borders of 4" (10 cm) on the sides and 2" (5 cm) on the top and bottom. This will make a template 8" × 20" (20 × 50 cm).

3 Using a tape measure or long ruler, start at one end of the wall and first make a mark against the ceiling or cornice 4" (10 cm) from the edge. Then continue to make marks at 16" (40 cm) intervals. These will represent the vertical stripes.

4 Using a plumb line to ensure that the stripes are absolutely vertical, make corresponding marks at the bottom of the wall. Position the chalk line between the two marks and snap it to draw in the lines.

5 Stick small squares of card to the corners at the back of the template to lift it away from the wall while painting. Position the template at the top of the wall between the first two chalk lines, and secure it in place with plastic putty or low-tack double-sided tape.

6 Mix a glaze by adding equal quantities of acrylic scumble glaze and water to the water-based paint in your chosen color.
A glaze will remain wet for longer, allowing you to join up the sections of the template.

7 Apply glaze with the 2" (50 mm) decorators' brush, running the side of the brush in a straight line against the inner edges of the template and then filling in the middle.

8 Lift the template and place it directly below and slightly overlapping the last working, still lining it up between the chalk lines. Repeat the last step and continue in this way until you reach the bottom of the wall, blending in each join as you go along.

9 To fill in the gaps that have been left at the top and bottom of the wall, hold a piece of card or a ruler against the edge of the stripe, angled away from the wall, and fill in the area with glaze.

10 Continue this process (from steps 5–9) along the wall until all the stripes have been painted. When the paint has dried, wash off the chalk lines with a damp cloth.

Stripes create a subtle background in this bedroom, which evokes a bygone era.

A simple gingham fabric has inspired the painting of these accessories.

SHOPPING LIST

MATERIALS

White water-based wall paint for the base

Universal stainers or artists' acrylic paints in your chosen colors

Acrylic scumble glaze

Water

Matte acrylic varnish

EQUIPMENT

1" (25 mm) flat nylon artists' brushes

Brush for varnish

Water-soluble pencils in the colors of the checks

Low-tack masking tape

Ruler

Protective latex gloves

Plastic or canvas drop cloths to protect surfaces

CHECKS

For this project, we have chosen a gingham fabric as inspiration. The main colors are a subtle blue and green, and a third color is created where the checks overlap. The background has a tea-stained color which is achieved by applying a very diluted antiquing glaze over the painted checks.

1 If necessary, prepare the surface and apply two coats of the base color (in this case, white).

2 Decide on the size of the checks and measure out the lines, marking them with a water-soluble pencil. Draw in all the lines in one direction first.

3 Mask off these stripes with low-tack masking tape, rubbing down the edges with your thumb nail to stop the glaze from bleeding under the tape.

4 Mix glazes in the two colors of the checks using artists' acrylic paint, scumble glaze and water. The glaze must be very transparent, so use more scumble glaze than water to dilute it.

Using the flat nylon brush, apply the first color glaze between the tape lines. Drag the brush through the glaze to give a fabric texture. Allow to dry and remove the tape.

5 When the glaze is dry, mask off the stripes in the opposite direction, pressing the tape down firmly. Then paint the entire stripe with the second glaze. (Where the two glazes cross, darker checks will be formed.)

6 Allow the second glaze to dry and then remove the masking tape slowly and carefully so as not to pull off the first layer of glaze.

7 Make a very transparent antiquing glaze using raw umber artists' acrylic or universal stainer mixed with scumble glaze and water. Paint an even layer over the entire surface to give a tea-stained effect.

8 When the glaze has dried, varnish over the surface with matte acrylic varnish.

WHITE-ON-WHITE TRELLIS

SHOPPING LIST

MATERIALS

White oil- or water-based wall paint in the base color
Oil- or water-based scumble glaze
Universal stainer in raw umber
Terebine driers (if using oil-based paints)
Mineral spirits (if using oil-based paints)
Water (for water-based paints)

EQUIPMENT

2" (50 mm) decorators' brush or a short-haired roller for base coat
Fine artists' fitch or brush
Stipple brush (hog softener)
Flat nylon artists' brushes
Masking tape
Ruler
Water-soluble pencil
Set square
Craft knife
Cloths to wipe brushes
Protective latex gloves
Plastic or canvas drop cloths to protect surfaces

This is a simple technique and an effective way of simulating real trellis. It can be done on any flat surface where real trellis could be placed. Versailles planter boxes frequently have trellis as a decorative feature on their sides. In this demonstration we have chosen white on white. However it can be done in any colors of your choice, using the same principle. The size of the trellis can vary according to the size of the object. The standard size of trellis is 4" × 4" (10 × 10 cm). In this example, the planes of the obelisk are small, so the size of the trellis is only 2½" × 2½" (6 × 6 cm) so as to be in proportion.

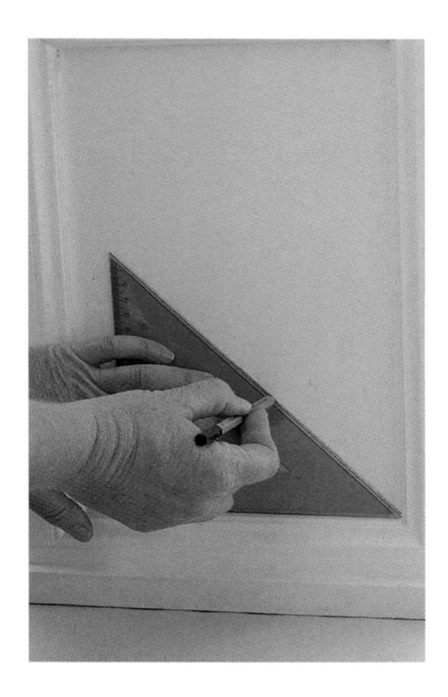

1 Complete the required surface preparation and apply two coats of white oil- or water-based paint, using either a brush or a short-haired roller, depending on the size of the area to be painted.

2 Measure the trellis. Place the set square in the bottom corner of the panel and draw a line at a 45-degree angle from one corner to the other. This line must be drawn lightly as it will be removed later—it is the center line to position the tape. Repeat this from all four corners to create the pattern. If you are working on a large object, draw a line down the middle and make sure your trellis pattern lines up with this center line.

3 The width of your masking tape determines the width of the slats of the trellis. The line you have just drawn indicates the center of the tape (representing the width of the slat). Measure and draw two lines on either side of the center line to give the full width of the tape.
A diamond shape will be created in the middle of this pattern. This is the size of the gap between the slats of the trellis. Using these measurements continue the pattern on the whole area to be trellised.

4 Take a small damp cloth and wipe out the center line.

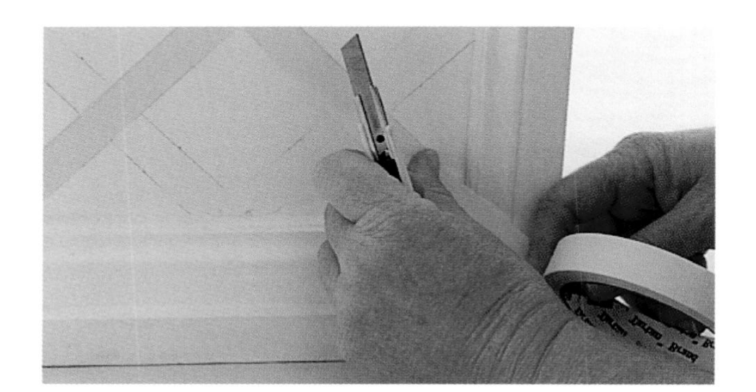

5 Stick the masking tape onto the trellis pattern between the lines you have drawn. Now rub your nail along the edges of the tape to secure it and stop the glaze from seeping underneath. Use a craft knife to cut the tape at the end of each line.

6 The glaze required for this project must be very transparent. In order to achieve this, mix the glaze using more scumble than paint (approximately five parts scumble glaze to two parts of white paint) and add a few drops of raw umber universal stainer to make a shadow glaze. Mix enough glaze using this proportion to fill in the diamond shapes between the masking tape.

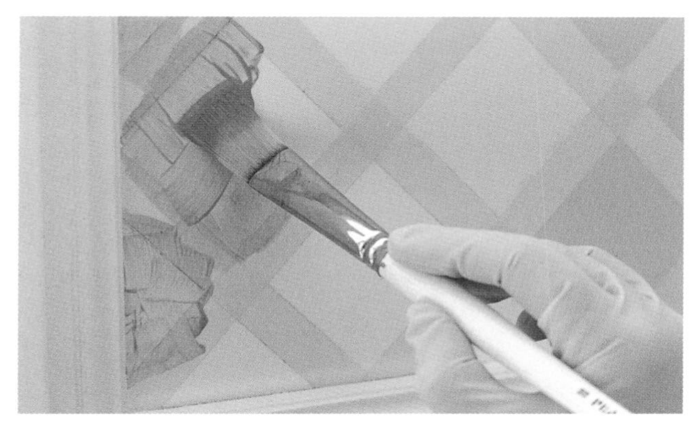

7 Using a flat nylon artists' brush, apply a thin coat of glaze to each square, working from the taped edges into the middle to prevent bleeding. Depending on the size of the pattern, do two or three blocks at a time.

8 The next step is to smooth out the brush strokes. Stipple the two or three blocks previously painted, wiping the stipple brush frequently on a cloth to prevent glaze from being picked up on the brush, which results in a coarse stipple. Clean any edges before the glaze dries.

9 To make the trellis look more realistic, shadow lines are added. Decide which 'slats' of the trellis are going to be on top as these will cast a darker shadow on the lower slats. Leave the tape on the upper 'slats' and remove it from the lower 'slats' (not illustrated).

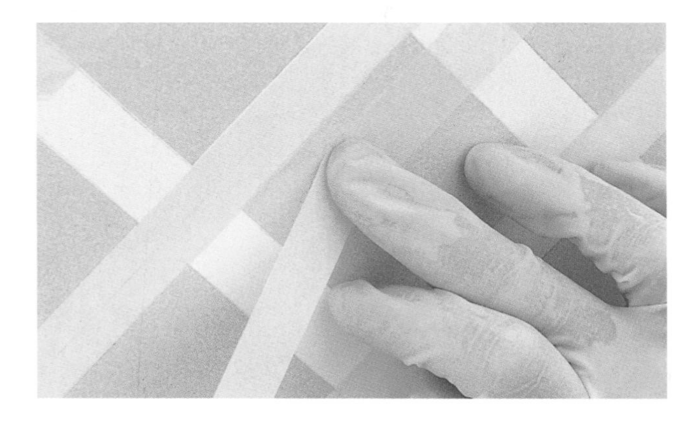

10 If you are not confident about doing the shadow line without a guide, stick new tape below the lower edge of the remaining tape, leaving a gap of approximately ¼" (5 mm).

Add a few more drops of universal stainer in raw umber to your glaze to make a darker shadow glaze.

11 Paint the glaze into the gap between the tape, then stipple it with a hog softener.

12 Using a fine artists' brush, paint a thin, soft glaze line on the top of the lower slat to indicate a slight shadow. Allow the paint to dry completely.

13 Remove the tape from the slats you have been working on and stick new masking tape to the lower slats to repeat the process, continuing until all the trellis is shaded in the same way.

Obelisks decorated with faux trellising create an attractive garden feature.

MURALS

Murals are painted artworks used to embellish interiors or exteriors of buildings, as opposed to pictures that hang on walls. Painted architectural features, such as windows, alcoves or columns, provide a focal point in a room, while an illusion of space can be created by painting a trompe l'oeil view through a window or arch. Simple murals in children's rooms bring to life favorite characters that are easily reproduced by tracing, copying or using an overhead or slide projector.

DRAWING A MURAL

SHOPPING LIST

EQUIPMENT

- **Tape measure**
- **Plumb line**
- **Chalk line**
- **Carpenter's level**
- **Water-soluble pencil**
- **String**
- **12" (30 cm) ruler**
- **Long ruler or set square**
- **Pencil and tracing paper or a photocopy of the chosen design**
- **Soft cloth**

PREPARATION AND GETTING STARTED

Once you have chosen a design for your mural the next step is to transfer the image, enlarged to the correct size, from the paper onto the wall or surface. If you are not confident enough to draw it freehand, there are a number of easy methods to transfer a design. These include scale drawing, using an overhead projector or a slide projector, and using photocopies and a tracing wheel. Each method is described in detail below, together with a list of equipment required for the specific method.

SCALE DRAWING

This is the simplest way to transfer a design and it does not need much equipment.

1 Using a pencil and set square, draw a grid over the design, making the blocks approximately 1" × 1" (25 × 25 mm). The actual size will vary depending on the original size of the design. The bigger the design, the bigger the blocks.

2 Enlarge the blocks proportionately and measure them onto the surface to be painted. (Use a plumb line to ensure that vertical lines are accurate.) Vertical lines can be made with a chalk line (or by chalking a length of string). With the help of another person, hold the chalk line taut up against the plumb line and snap it against the wall.

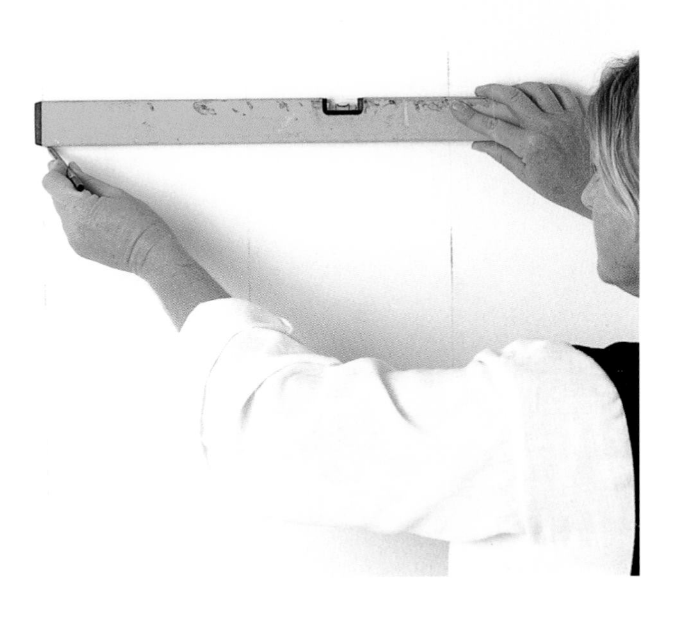

3 Measure out the horizontal lines and draw them in; use a carpenter's level to check that they are accurate.

4 Using a water-soluble pencil, transfer the design from the paper to the wall by copying the design block for block. When the entire design is drawn onto the surface, use a soft cloth to remove the chalk lines of the grid.

SHOPPING LIST

EQUIPMENT

Overhead or slide projector

Transparent film or 35 mm slide

Marker pen

Water-soluble pencil or charcoal

USING A SLIDE OR OVERHEAD PROJECTOR

A slide projector or an overhead projector (OHP) is useful when doing large murals. A small color slide can be enlarged by projection to fill an entire wall, or a design can be traced or copied onto transparent sheets and projected to any size.

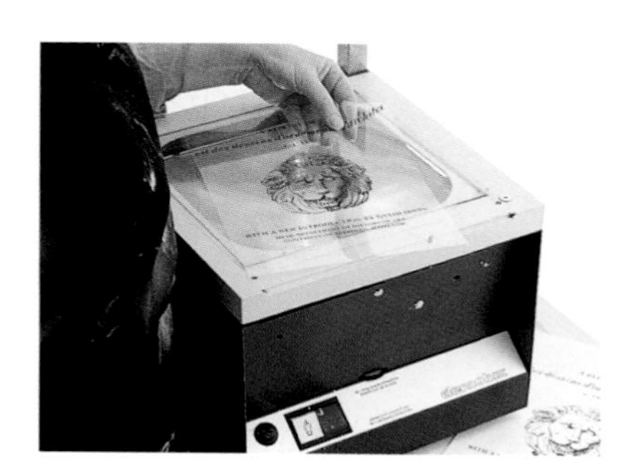

1 If using an OHP, place the transparent film over the design and trace it using the marker pen. If you have access to a copy shop, you could have the design photocopied onto a transparency, which would give you a more accurate rendition.

2 Project the image onto the wall, adjusting the position of the machine until you achieve the correct size. (The size of the enlargement will depend on the distance between the wall and the projector.) Adjust the focus until the image is sharp. Using the water-soluble pencil or charcoal, draw over the lines projected onto the wall.

SHOPPING LIST

EQUIPMENT

Paper, pencil, water-soluble pencil

Cutting mat

Tracing wheel

Transparent adhesive tape

Masking tape

T-shirt fabric

Cotton batting

Chalk or charcoal powder

Sandpaper (220 grit)

PHOTOCOPY AND TRACING WHEEL METHOD

This is an easy and quick way of reproducing any design onto a surface and is always accurate. Once you have chosen your design, measure the area where you intend to place it to determine the size of the enlargement.

Most standard photocopy machines can enlarge by degrees and can print on 11" x 17" (280 x 430 mm) size paper. If your original design is larger than 11" x 17", you might have to divide it in half or quarters, enlarge each of the pieces separately and then stick them together. Some copy shops have the facility to print on larger paper sizes and their machines can adjust an enlargement to the size you require in one action. Have a few copies made so that you have a backup if any copies get damaged in the process of tracing.

1 Once you have your design on paper, place it on a cutting mat and follow the lines of the design with a tracing wheel. Apply enough pressure to perforate the surface without tearing the paper. If the paper tears, repair it with transparent tape and trace over it again.

2 Turn the design over and, on the reverse side, lightly sand over the perforated line with 220 grit sandpaper to remove the paper burr and open up the holes.

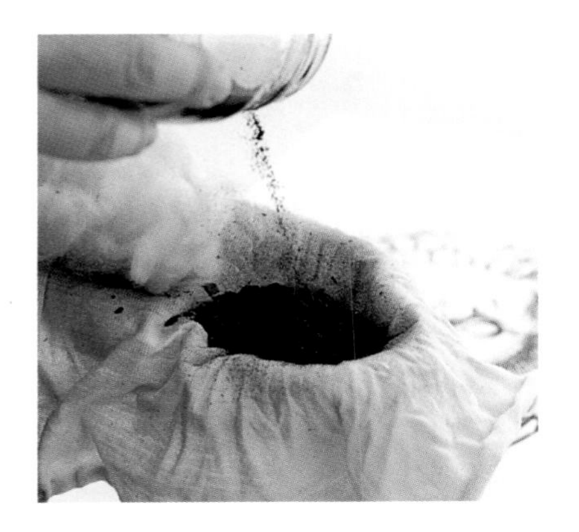

3 Make a pounce pad by placing a square of T-shirt material in the palm of your cupped hand and filling it with chalk or charcoal powder. Cover it with a wad of upholsterers' batting and close the fabric around it, making a soft pad. Close the back of the pad with masking tape or a rubber band.

4 Position the design on the surface and secure it with masking tape. Pat the pounce pad over the design allowing the powder to come out in a fine layer. Rub over the powdery surface with the pad, forcing the chalk or charcoal through the holes and onto the surface behind.

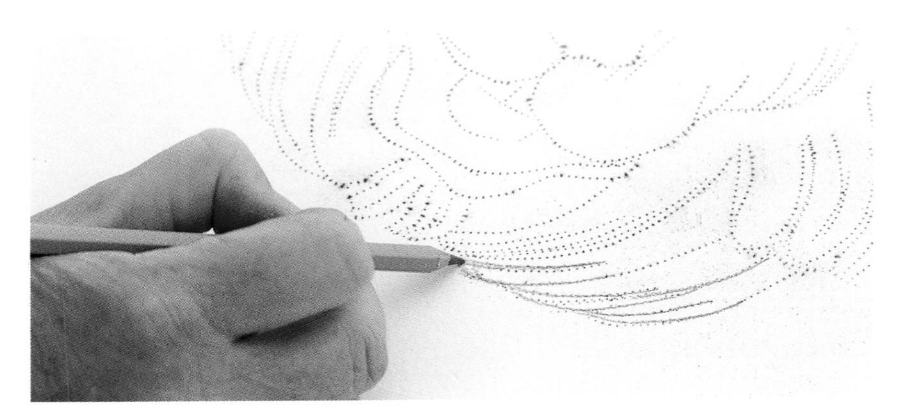

5 When the paper is removed, a fine line of powder dots will remain on the surface, indicating the outline of the design.

If you are working on a smooth surface, such as a wall painted with an oil-based paint, the dots could rub off easily when you start painting, so it is advisable to draw over the dots with a water-soluble pencil and then dust off the powder with a dusting brush.

If the surface is acrylic-coated and you have used charcoal powder, which is more intense and sticks better than chalk, you do not need to draw over it, merely dust off the excess charcoal.

FAUX BALUSTRADE

SHOPPING LIST

MATERIALS

Oil-based:

White eggshell wall paint

Oil-based scumble glaze

Artists' oils in raw umber, black

Mineral spirits

Water-based:

White acrylic wall paint

Acrylic scumble glaze

Acrylics in raw umber, black

EQUIPMENT

2" (50 mm) decorators' brush for base coat and for applying shadow glaze

1" (25 mm) decorators' brush for darker glaze and for mixing

Hog softener for blending, shading

Artists' fitch for highlighting details

Thick card, masonite or plywood cut into the outline of a top rail, baluster and base

Full-size copies of baluster pattern, and reduced-size copies as a guide (the number of copies will depend on the size of the area)

Pencil and tracing paper

Paper and a soft pencil for shading

Plumb line

Measuring tape

Protective latex gloves

Plastic or canvas drop cloths to protect surfaces

Shading is the most effective way of achieving a three-dimensional look, as a shadow placed under an object immediately lifts it up. A circle drawn on a piece of paper becomes a ball when shading is put in. Scumble glaze mixed with paint creates the transparency needed to make shadows look authentic, as it allows edges to be softened and tones to be blended from lightest to the darkest. Painting a balustrade can be done directly onto a wall or on cutouts that are then fixed to a wall. The base coat can be any light color you choose, in either oil or acrylic.

1 Find a catalogue of balustrading styles for an elevation, and have a photocopy made to the final size you require. The full size of the baluster will be approximately 22" (57 cm) without the top rail or base. Using a reduced-size photocopy, decide which direction the light is coming from, and put in the shading on the opposite side. Use a soft (4B) pencil to do this.

2 Scale up the baluster and draw or transfer it to the required size. Decide on the spacing between the balusters—this is normally 12" (30 cm) from center to center. Mark the position of the balusters on the wall, making sure they are vertical. A plumb line can be dropped down to ensure this. Trace the balusters onto the wall or board. If using board, each baluster will have to be cut out individually.

3 Prepare two glazes using white base coat, scumble glaze, raw umber and a small amount of black. Thin down with the appropriate thinner. Use a plate to mix in between shades of lighter and darker gray.

4 Paint the entire baluster with a pale gray, almost white, glaze. Stipple (soften) with a hog softener to eliminate brush marks.

5 Using the small shaded photocopy as a guide, paint the dark gray glaze down the side opposite the light source and under the rounded sections. Also paint a little dark glaze down the lighter side, then wipe out a strong highlight. Blend in the shadows with the hog softener (also called a stippler). The more you stipple the lighter it gets.

6 The final step only takes place when everything is completely dry. Use an artists' fitch and the lightest glaze to put a highlight on all the balusters, then soften them with the hog softener.

Simple shading gives depth and form, creating an illusion of reality.

PAINTED CLOUDS

SHOPPING LIST

MATERIALS

Oil-based:

White eggshell wall paint

Oil-based scumble glaze

Artists' oils in ultramarine or cobalt blue, raw sienna, white and alizarin crimson

Mineral spirits

Water-based:

White acrylic wall paint

Acrylic scumble glaze

Artists' acrylics in ultramarine or cobalt blue, raw sienna, white and alizarin crimson

Water

EQUIPMENT

Brushes:

2" (50 mm) decorators' brush for laying on glazes

1" (25 mm) decorators' brush for shading clouds

Hog softener

6" (15 cm) hake or badger brush for softening clouds

Water-soluble pencil

Paper towels or soft cloths

Protective latex gloves

Plastic or canvas drop cloths to protect surfaces

Painted on a ceiling, a blue sky with a few clouds scattered about can be very effective, creating a feeling of space and a sense of height. If you don't have the confidence to paint a big area, a smaller panel, such as a faux skylight painted onto the ceiling, works well. Alternatively, you could paint clouds on a separate wooden or canvas panel that is later applied to the ceiling. Dark clouds can create a somber atmosphere, whereas introducing a small amount of pink or yellow lightens the effect. The surface to be painted should be as smooth as possible.

1 The first step is to make a scale drawing of the space you want to paint and then block in the cloud shapes. A scale of 1" to 1' (2.5 to 30 cm) works well. If you have a photograph or a watercolor sketch to copy, it will make the task much easier.

For the sky, mix a soft blue glaze using ultramarine or cobalt blue mixed with white. Then mix a white glaze for the clouds. For gray shading in the clouds, mix raw sienna with ultramarine and white glaze (add a little alizarin crimson for pinkish tones). Quantities will depend on the size of the area to be painted.

2 Transfer the drawing from the squared-up design to the ceiling, or draw in the clouds freehand using a water-soluble pencil.

3 Paint in the sky areas with blue glaze and stipple out the brush strokes. Wipe the edges of the clouds clean with a paper towel or cloth.

4 Paint in the clouds completely with white glaze, then work the gray shadow color into the white glaze, adding extra color where necessary. Remember that the edge of a cloud should be lighter than its body. Stipple to blend the colors.

5 Extra softening and blending can be done with a wide hake or badger brush.

Create an illusion of light and space with a view through a faux skylight.

GRISAILLE

SHOPPING LIST

MATERIALS

(This technique can be done in either oil- or water-based paint or glaze)
Medium-gray wall paint for base
Artists' oils or acrylics in gray, ivory, black, raw umber, titanium white
Scumble glaze
Mineral spirits or water

EQUIPMENT

Roller or wide decorators' brush for base coat
Fine round artists' brushes
Hog softener and a round fitch brush for stippling
Dusting brush
Water-soluble pencil
Tracing wheel
Masking tape
Sandpaper (220 grit)
T-shirt fabric, cotton batting and chalk or charcoal powder to make a pounce bag
Paper towels or soft cloths
Protective latex gloves
Plastic or canvas drop cloths to protect surfaces

Grisaille, a French word meaning 'grayness', refers to painting in monochromatic shades of gray. It is a trompe l'oeil technique whereby three-dimensional (3-D) forms are painted onto a flat surface using white as a highlight, with shades of gray getting gradually darker in the shadow areas. As a technique, monochrome shading is a good training to help you master more complicated full-color trompe l'oeil murals. It can be used effectively in rendering plaster relief work, as a decorative cartouche on door panels or above a doorway, or for wall panels. Designs are readily available from reference books, but keep in mind that the grisaille technique is usually used to simulate architectural detail or relief stone carving.

1 Prepare the surface and apply two coats of gray for the base.

2 When you have chosen your design, photocopy it and enlarge it to the required size. Have a few copies made so that you can use them to practice shading and to test the colors before you begin working.

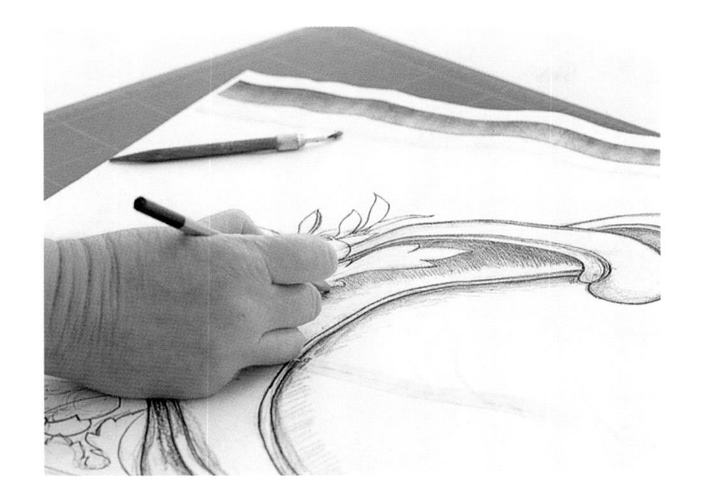

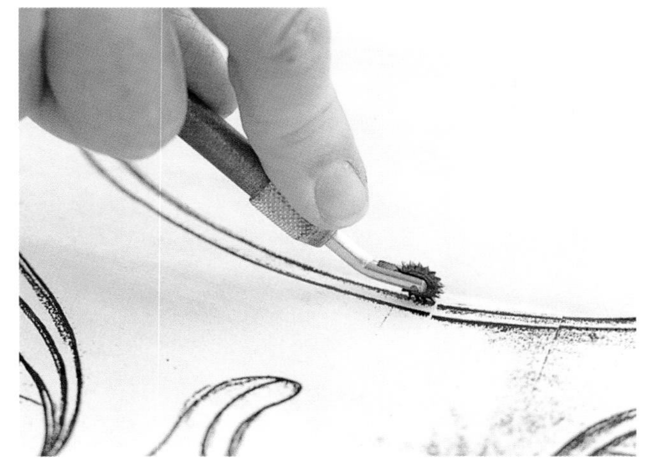

3 Use a copy of the design to plan the shading. Decide where the light source will be on your design. In reality, light normally comes from a window or an overhead light, so the safest option is to have the light coming from either the top left or top right corner.

With the pencil, shade all the areas that would be in dark shadow. This will immediately give the picture a 3-D effect and help to guide you when you start painting.

4 To transfer your design to the surface you intend painting, follow the instructions on photocopying and tracing in the introduction to murals (see pp60–61).

Place your design on a cutting mat and run the tracing wheel along the design, making small pin-holes in the paper. Lightly sand the back to open the holes further.

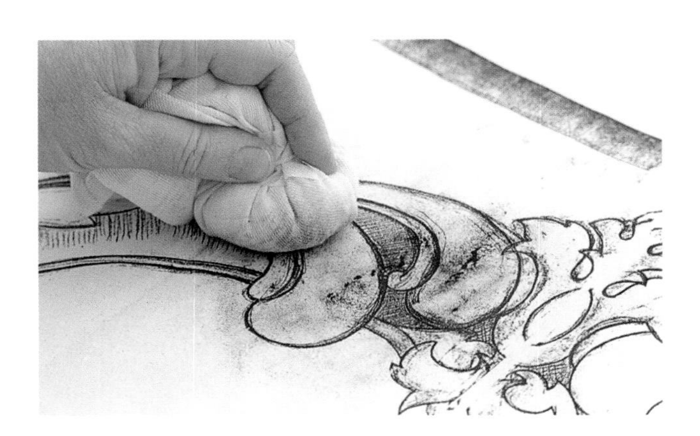

5 Position the design and hold it in place with masking tape. Make a pounce pad filled with chalk or charcoal powder (see p61) and tap it over the design, forcing the powder through the holes. Remove the design and, if the dots are not very clear, draw over the design with a water-soluble pencil.

6 Mix three glazes for the shadows and highlights using equal quantities of artists' oil or acrylic paints, scumble glaze and solvent. (See p18 for recipes.)

Using the base color as the mid-tone gray, you will need to mix one dark glaze for the darkest shadows, one glaze that is lighter than the base color, and one that is almost white for the highlights.

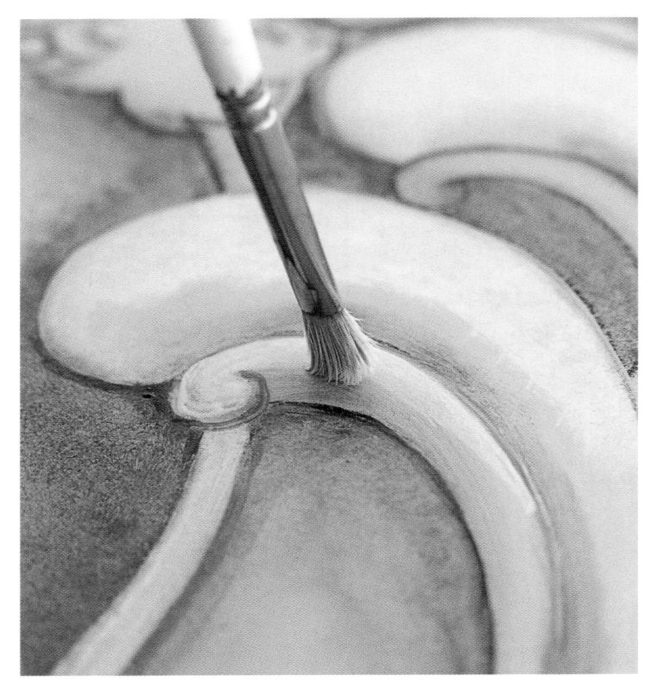

7 Using your drawing as a reference, start by painting in the darkest shadows with a round artists' brush, then stipple with a hog softener to soften the edges. Have a clean cloth on hand to wipe off any areas that might get overworked and to keep your stipple brush clean.

8 Using the lighter pale gray glaze, apply narrow patches of highlights to areas that are raised in the design. Keep in mind that the base color is the middle tone and must be visible between the shadows and highlights. Stipple to soften the edges (use a round fitch brush in areas where the hog softener will be too large). Allow to dry.

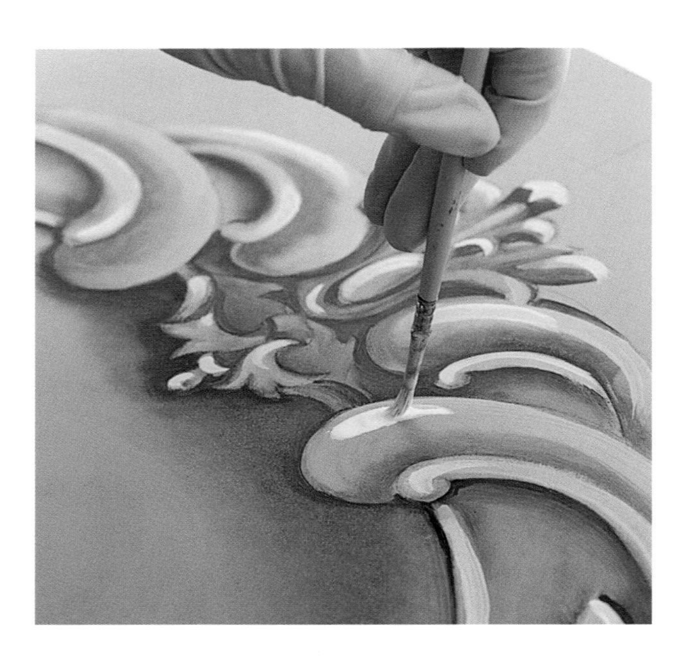

9 Apply the white highlight glaze on top of the previous working. This highlight will occur only in small areas, indicating where the light would catch the highest points of the molding.

Grisaille and trompe l'oeil (see p70) give a 3-D effect to a fire screen set against a faux stone-blocked fireplace.

TROMPE L'OEIL FAUX PANELS

SHOPPING LIST

MATERIALS

Oil-based:

- **Eggshell wall paint in a pale color**
- **Oil-based scumble glaze**
- **Artists' oils or universal stainers in raw umber, black and white**
- **Mineral spirits**

Water-based:

- **Acrylic paint in a pale color**
- **Water-based scumble glaze**
- **Artists' acrylics or universal stainers in raw umber, black and white**
- **Water**

EQUIPMENT

- **2" (50 mm) decorators' brush or roller for base coat**
- **Flat nylon artists' brush**
- **Hog softener**
- **Ruler**
- **Set square**
- **Water-soluble pencil**
- **Craft board or cardboard**
- **Craft knife**
- **Low-tack masking tape**
- **Protective latex gloves**
- **Plastic or canvas drop cloths to protect surfaces**

An effective way of making a flat surface look more interesting is to paint panels on it, giving it a three-dimensional appearance. Trompe l'oeil, meaning to trick the eye, is the term used for this effect. Panels can be painted on doors, walls, cupboards or below a dado rail, and they can be simple or elaborate, with raised moldings, recesses and beveled edges. If you are working on a door, remove it from its hinges and rest it on a table or trestles before you paint it. Start with something simple and work with muted shades. Once you have mastered the principles of trompe l'oeil-shaded panels, the technique can be done on any surface that has previously been paint finished. Panels are effective on a marble or wood grain finish.

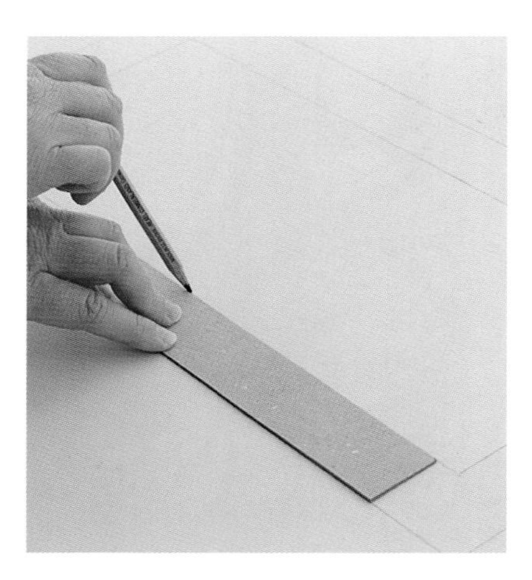

1 Prepare the surface and apply two coats of the base color. Once you have decided on a design and the proportions of the main panels, draw them onto the surface. Then draw in the internal panel by cutting a cardboard strip the correct width and use it as a template. The template used here is 1½" (40 mm).

2 If working on a colored base coat, mix four shadow glazes, graded from off-white to tones of brownish gray. The glazes are tones obtained by adding a little of the darkest color to some of the white. Follow the recipes given on p18 for mixing glazes.

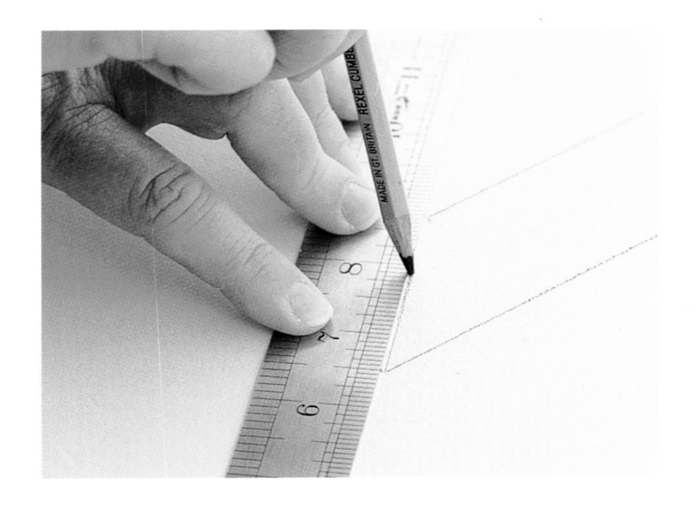

3 To get mitered corners, draw a 45-degree angle between the two planes. Decide where the light is coming from, for example, the top left. This will determine the position of the shadows on the panels. The lightest part of the panel is always directly opposite the darkest—usually the top and bottom planes. The second lightest part is at right angles to the others (on the side of the light source).

4 Begin working on two opposite planes, the lightest and the darkest. (You cannot work simultaneously on adjacent planes as they will smudge.) Use low-tack tape to mask off the lightest plane (the one at the top) on the outside of the lines you have drawn, including mitering the corners. Then mask off the darkest plane (the one at the bottom), again on the outside of the lines and on the outside of the mitered corners.

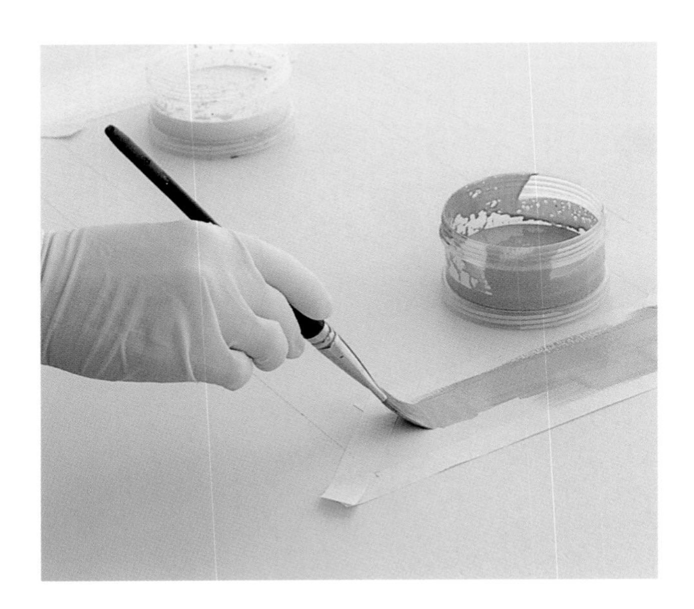

5 Apply the darkest glaze to the bottom section of the panel and the lightest glaze to the top section. Use a flat nylon brush to get a smooth, even flow of glaze.

6 Stipple the surface with the hog softener to eliminate the brush strokes and create an even shadow. Wipe the brush frequently to remove excess glaze.

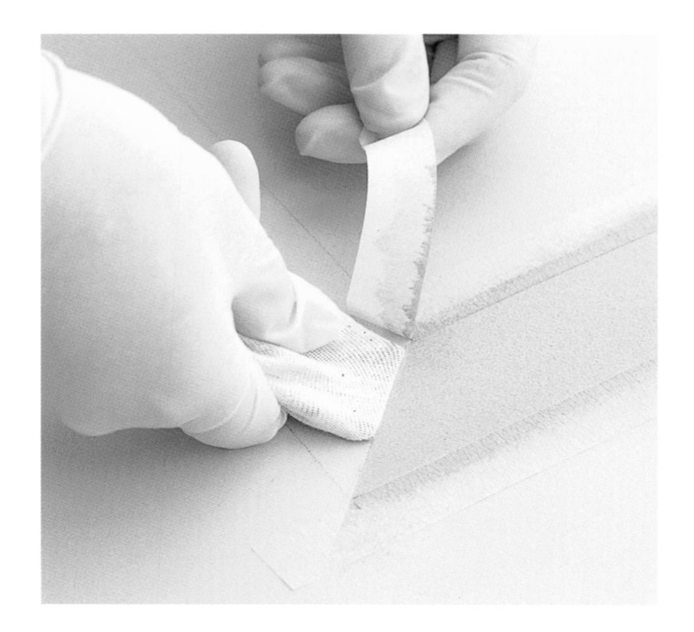

7 As soon as you finish stippling, carefully remove the tape and clean the edges. If glaze has bled under the tape, wipe it off with a piece of soft cloth wrapped over a small piece of firm board, to leave a clean edge.

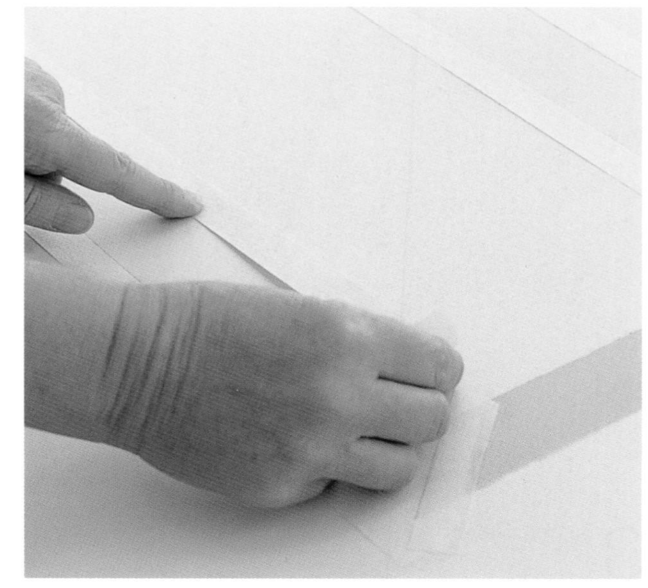

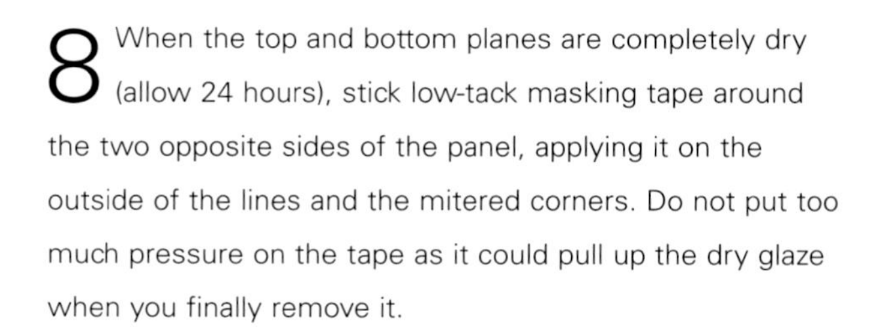

8 When the top and bottom planes are completely dry (allow 24 hours), stick low-tack masking tape around the two opposite sides of the panel, applying it on the outside of the lines and the mitered corners. Do not put too much pressure on the tape as it could pull up the dry glaze when you finally remove it.

9 Apply the second darkest glaze thinly and evenly at right angles to the darkest shadow (on the side furthest from the light source). Repeat on the other side of the panel with the off-white glaze. Stipple to soften as in Step 6.

10 When both sides are finished, remove the tape carefully so as not to lift up the dry glazes on the corners. Allow at least 24 hours for it to dry completely, then varnish with either matte or gloss varnish.

You can't pick up your coat and walk out of this door—they are both painted using trompe l'oeil techniques.

DECOUPAGE

SHOPPING LIST

MATERIALS

- Water-based wall paint in the color of your choice
- Selection of pictures and borders
- Wallpaper glue
- Matte-finish water-based varnish
- Water

EQUIPMENT

- Roller or decorators' brush for base coats
- Foam applicator
- Large commercial sponge
- Water-soluble pencil
- Carpenter's level
- Cutting mat
- Craft knife and sharp scissors
- Metal ruler and set square
- Low-tack putty or masking tape
- Protective latex gloves
- Plastic or canvas drop cloths to protect surfaces

Decoupage is an old tradition of decorating with cutout pictures glued to small objects, boxes, trays or furniture. During the 18th century, the art of decoupage was extended to larger formats and the print room came into being. Here, etchings or souvenirs of travels abroad were stuck directly to a wall instead of being framed. Print rooms have become fashionable again and this is an easy and inexpensive way of decorating a small room, passage or hallway. The prints are traditionally black and white and show up well on a dark background. Some decorating shops sell special prints and rolls of border patterns specifically for the creation of a print room. An alternative is to find suitable designs in Victorian reference books, which are copyright free, and have them enlarged to suit your requirements.

1 Prepare the wall surface well and paint with two coats of water-based paint in a suitable color. There must be no imperfections or bumps on the surface as this will show under the prints. (An oil-based surface is not suitable as it will be too smooth to hold the glue.)

2 Cut out the prints and borders. Measure the sides of the main print to determine the length of the border strips, which will make up the picture frame. Miter the corners to 45° using a set square. Cut out any bows or tassels that you are going to use to finish off the project.

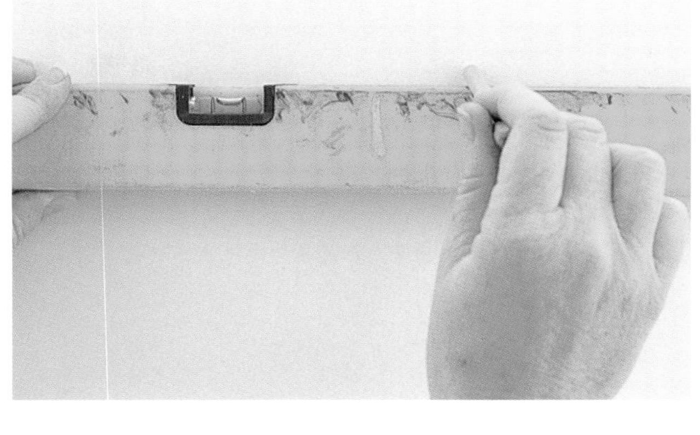

3 Decide how you are going to arrange the prints on the wall and measure up the positions. Work outward from the center of the wall and position the prints with low-tack putty or masking tape. Use a carpenter's level and plumb line to ensure that the print will be straight. Lightly mark the center top and center bottom position points of the print using a water-soluble pencil.

4 Remove the center print and turn it face-down onto a clean working surface. Take off the low-tack tape and spread a thin layer of wallpaper glue, using the foam applicator to get an even layer.

5 Wet the commercial sponge with water, squeeze out the excess and keep it handy. Lift the print up carefully and place it on the wall in the position you have marked.

6 Take the damp sponge and gently but quickly wipe over the surface, smoothing it out and removing any air bubbles. The print will appear to be wrinkled but will flatten as it dries. Do not overwork the sponging, as it will damage the print.

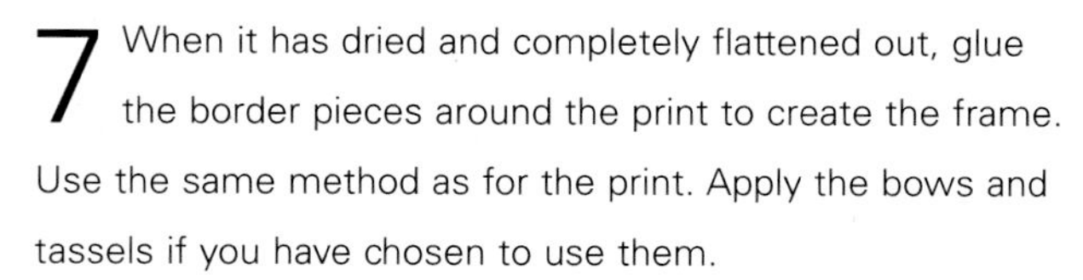

7 When it has dried and completely flattened out, glue the border pieces around the print to create the frame. Use the same method as for the print. Apply the bows and tassels if you have chosen to use them.

8 It is essential to varnish all decoupage prints with a matte water-based varnish to protect them.

The pale walls of this intimate oval dining room make a perfect backdrop for a print room.

WOOD GRAINING

Wood graining, one of the oldest decorative paint finishes, was once practiced by travelling master craftsmen who went from town to town 'wood graining' doors, wall panels, mantelpieces and church pews to simulate costly woods such as oak or mahogany. Today only a few original examples remain in historic houses and churches. The fashion for painted wood graining periodically declines but has recently revived because of the shortage of beautiful wood.

RUBBER ROCKER TECHNIQUE

SHOPPING LIST

MATERIALS

Oil-based wall paint in dark brown for base color

White oil-based wall paint

Scumble glaze

Mineral spirits

Satin varnish

EQUIPMENT

Decorators' brush or roller to apply the base color

2" (50 mm) decorators' brush for glaze

Rubber rocker (heart grainer) with a large grain

Flogger brush

Metal graining combs

Paper towel

Protective latex gloves

Plastic or canvas drop cloths to protect surfaces

NOTE: This technique can also be done in water-based paint and glaze. As they dry faster than oil-based materials, skill and speed are required.

A rubber rocker, or heart graining tool, is the most frequently used piece of equipment to create a variety of faux wood grains. It takes some practice to learn all its possibilities but once you have mastered it, you can have a lot of fun creating some convincing and accurate faux grains. By changing the base color of your surface, a multitude of fantasy wood grains can be created.

1 Prepare the surface and apply two coats of the dark brown paint, or your own choice of color, for the base coat.

2 Mix a glaze using equal parts of white paint, scumble glaze and mineral spirits (see p18 for recipe).

3 Apply the white glaze to the surface in vertical stripes approximately 12" (30 cm) wide using the 2" (50 mm) decorators' brush.

4 Take a piece of crumpled paper towel and, with both hands, drag it over the surface to wipe off excess glaze and at the same time create a streaked grain in the glaze.

5 Starting at the top end of the surface, hold the rubber rocker (heart grainer) with both hands in the middle. Hold one edge against the surface with your hands angled away from you and your arms extended.

6 Drag the rocker down towards you while slowly rolling it back and forth, creating the grain pattern. To make a long grain, rock with a slow gradual movement. A short grain will require a more rapid and frequent rocking motion.

7 Wipe the excess glaze from the grooves in the rocker. Place it at the top of the surface, next to the previous working and drag it down again, keeping the lines parallel. To avoid a repetition in the grain, turn the rocker over with each new line. You should do two to three lines in a 12" (30 cm) strip.

8 Feel the metal comb to establish which is the smooth side and hold this side to the surface. Drag the comb vertically in parallel lines over the entire area to create a fine hairline grain over the heart grain.

9 To further refine the grain, go over the surface with a flogger brush. Flogging is a light slapping motion with the brush, working from the bottom of the surface up towards the top. Overworking this step will eliminate the grain completely, so be delicate.

10 Repeat from Step 3 until the whole object is done. When the glaze is dry, finish with a coat of varnish.

The colors of the wood grain finish enhance the found objects in this zen-influenced table setting.

SIMPLE PAINTED PINE

SHOPPING LIST

MATERIALS

Oil-based:

Wall paint in a pale wheat color for the base coat

Oil-based scumble glaze

Artists' oils in raw sienna, burnt sienna, yellow ochre, titanium white, raw umber and burnt umber for knots

Mineral spirits

Water-based:

Wall paint in a pale wheat color for the base coat

Acrylic scumble glaze

Artists' acrylics in raw sienna, burnt sienna, yellow ochre, titanium white, raw umber and burnt umber for knots

Water

Oil- or water-based varnish

EQUIPMENT

2" (50 mm) decorators' brush for base painting and laying on glaze

2" (50 mm) dragging brush with alternate bristles cut out (toothed), or an overgrainer

Small flat artists' brush for knots

Japanese hakes for softening

Protective latex gloves

Plastic or canvas drop cloths to protect surfaces.

The technique of wood graining can be used to simulate wood on a number of different surfaces, such as plastic, cement, chipboard, MDF board and plywood. The color and type of existing wood can also be altered. In Paris, many exterior doors, which were originally made of pine, have been painted to look like oak. Wood faux finishes can be so well done that one assumes they are natural and original. Whatever type of wood you choose to replicate, research is important. Collect pictures, take photographs and do sketches of different wood grains before you start. Antique shops are a good source of furniture made from various woods that are no longer readily available.

1 Apply the base coat, which should always be lighter than the glaze selected for the grain.

2 Using artists' colors, mix raw sienna, white and yellow ochre to the same color as the background, and add an equal amount of scumble glaze and the appropriate thinner for oil- or water-based paint to make a thin glaze.

3 Paint the surface with a thin layer of this glaze.

6 With the toothed dragging brush (or overgrainer) paint in the straight graining along each side of the figuring, following the shapes.

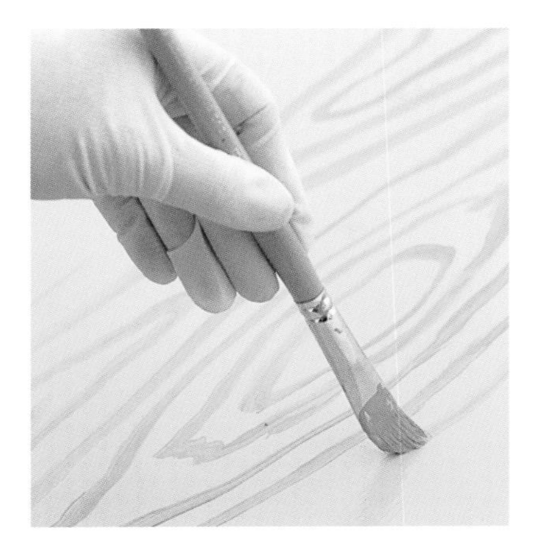

4 Mix a darker glaze and use the flat artists' bristle brush to paint in the basic shape of the figured graining and position the knots. Draw an amoeba (irregular) shape then draw bigger ones around it, getting more elongated and thicker towards the top and bottom. (Have a piece of grained wood handy to copy, or photographs of knots and patterns.)

7 Paint in the knots using a darker color (a mixture of burnt sienna and burnt umber). Knots are often oval shaped and angled upward. When the knot is dry, darker spots and circles can be painted inside it.

5 Using a wide hake, brush upward from the center of the 'amoeba' to elongate the markings, and down again the same way.

8 While the glaze is still wet, soften some areas around the knots with a Japanese hake.

9 Finish with a coat of clear oil- or water-based varnish. To obtain a bleached pine effect, add a little white paint to the varnish to make a 'milk varnish'.

MAHOGANY

SHOPPING LIST

MATERIALS

- Light terracotta wall paint for the base coat
- Oil- or water based:
- Oil or acrylic scumble glaze
- Artists' oils or acrylics in burnt sienna, burnt umber, raw umber
- Terebine driers (only used for first working)
- Mineral spirits
- Water
- Varnish

EQUIPMENT

- 2" (50 mm) and 1" (25 mm) decorators' brushes
- Flogging brush
- Badger softener or Japanese hake
- Overgrainer or artists' fitch
- Fine sandpaper (600 grit)
- Protective latex gloves
- Plastic or canvas drop cloths to protect surfaces

Mahogany, one of the most beautiful woods, is now very scarce. The color varies according to age and polish and is usually a rich dark red-brown. The most popular rendition of mahogany includes the heart wood (concentric oval shapes). It is astounding to see pressed wood cupboard doors painted in a terracotta/red base coat, being transformed with a paint brush into rich-grained mahogany. This technique can be done in oil- or water-based paints. We have done the first working in water-based paint for quick drying purposes. The second working is in oil-based paint and will take much longer to dry.

1 Prepare the surface well and apply two coats of paint in terracotta for the base color.

FIRST WORKING: ARTISTS' ACRYLICS

2 Mix burnt umber with water and acrylic scumble glaze to form a glaze with the consistency of thin cream. Paint a thin layer of this glaze onto the object. Allow the glaze to set slightly (no more than a few minutes) before you begin flogging.

3 Hold the flogging brush in an upright position and slap it against the panel in short overlapping movements, starting at the bottom and working up to the top. When a single brush-width panel has been flogged, turn the flogger over and use short strokes to fill in the gap below the starting point. Work quickly and do not overdo the flogging as this will eliminate all the marks. Leave to dry thoroughly.

SECOND WORKING: ARTISTS' OILS

4 Mix an oil-based glaze using burnt sienna with a small amount of raw umber, scumble glaze and mineral spirits so that the mixture has the consistency of thin cream. Use a flat brush to paint a thin layer of glaze over the whole panel.

5 Mix a very strong glaze, the same color as the previous glaze. (It must be almost pure artists' oil colors. A small amount of scumble glaze and mineral spirits can be added to make the glaze flow.) Dip the brush into a stronger color mix and hold the brush with your fingers underneath and your thumb on top.

6 Starting at the bottom with the edge of the brush on the panel, push the brush up, and bring it down again, making a small peaked oval shape.

Repeat this action three or four times, making more peaked ovals. They should be closer together at the base, getting further apart at the top.

7 Using a badger brush or Japanese hake, soften the effect by fanning out from the base of the oval to the top. This pulls out the heart grain.

8 Use an overgrainer or an artists' fitch to add grain on either side of heart grain. This new grain should run at a straight angle following the outside edge of the oval.

9 Finish by applying two coats of a good gloss or semi-gloss varnish. Sand lightly between coats with 600 grit sandpaper. When painting a number of panels or doors, vary the position of the heart grain, and do some with only straight graining, which could also run at a slight angle.

Painted faux mahogany paneling has been used to create a trompe l'oeil effect of doors in a display cabinet.

LIGHT OAK

SHOPPING LIST

MATERIALS

Base coat: white wall paint mixed with raw sienna and a little raw umber
Oil-based:
Eggshell or semi-gloss enamel mixed to the correct color
Oil-based scumble glaze
Artists' oils in raw sienna, burnt sienna and titanium white
Mineral spirits
Water-based:
Acrylic paint mixed to the correct color
Acrylic scumble glaze
Artists' acrylics in raw sienna, burnt sienna and titanium white
Water
Gloss or semi-gloss varnish

EQUIPMENT

2" (50 mm) and 1" (25 mm) decorators' brushes
Heart grain rubber rocker with comb or a triangular rubber comb
Artists' fitch
Overgrainer
Hog softener or Japanese hake
Fine steel comb
Check roller
Cardboard and soft cloth
Sandpaper (600 grit)
Protective latex gloves

Oak has been used for centuries for furniture, panelling and many other items. New oak is a light golden color, but it darkens with age to a mellow light tan or brown. The natural grain is very hard and is darker than the soft wood in-between. Fashion trends dictate color. At one time most oak furniture and architectural details were painted with Black Japan (a type of lacquer); but whitewashed, or limed, oak has always been popular. Oak is one of the most difficult woods to paint as the markings of the grain must be well observed and faithfully reproduced, so work from a sample or sketch.

1 Prepare and apply the base coat, which should always be lighter than the graining glaze.

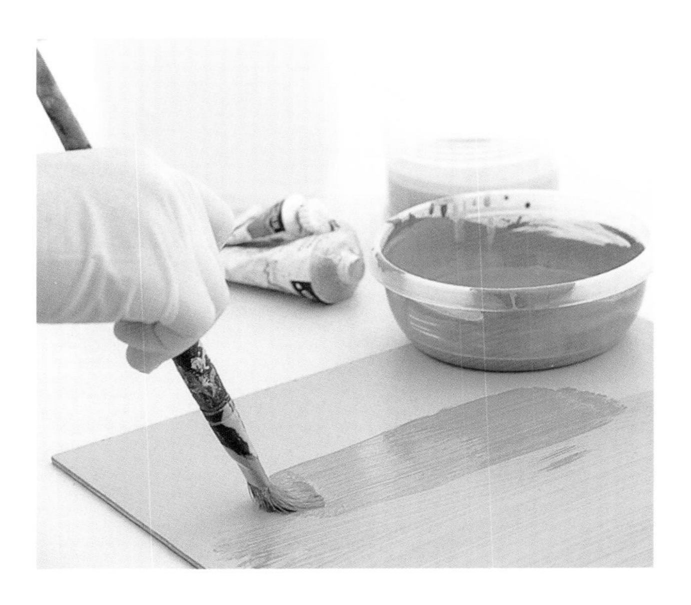

2 Make up a glaze for graining that is several shades darker than the background. Use raw sienna, a little titanium white and a touch of burnt sienna, and add scumble glaze and the appropriate thinner. Test it on a sample board.

3 Paint a thin layer of glaze on a section of the panel for the heart grain.

4 Take the heart grain rocker and, starting at the top of the panel, pull it downward, rocking it to and fro.

5 To make the straight grain, take the comb side of the rocker, or a triangular comb, and draw it down one side of the rocker pattern, following the grain, then down the other side. Additional grain markings can be put in at this stage, using the overgrainer or thin brushes. Soften slightly with a Japanese hake or hog softener if necessary.

6 Take the steel comb and pull it across the straight grain with short jerky strokes. This cuts the grain.

7 When the panel is dry, define the pore marks with a check roller (which is fed with raw umber glaze from a brush resting on the roller's serrated discs). Hold the brush on the roller and run it forward in the direction of the grain.

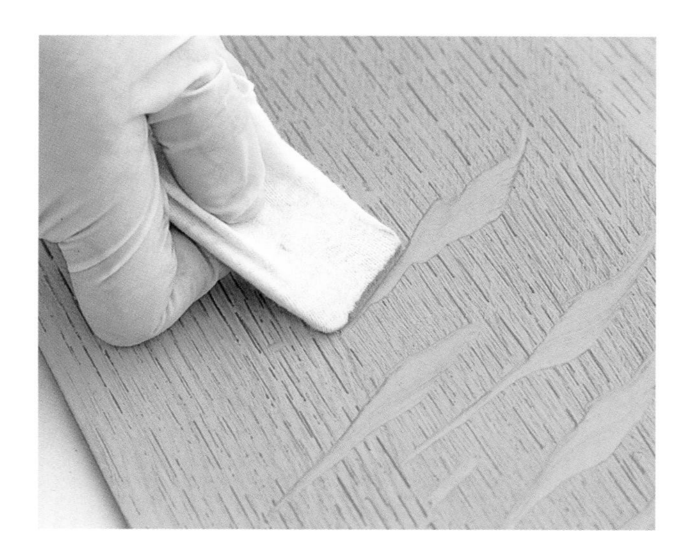

8 Cover a piece of cardboard with cloth and, using short tapering strokes, wipe out the glaze to form medullary rays, the characteristic 'flame' marks found in oak.

9 Protect the panels with two coats of gloss or semi-gloss varnish, sanding lightly between each coat with 600 grit paper.

A traditional wooden tea tray has been given a light oak finish.

STONE & MARBLE

Stone and marble faux finishes can be executed in a realistic way by copying the genuine item; matching the colors and replicating the veins and cracks that occur naturally. The technique is frequently used in restoration work when the real marble is either not obtainable or simply too expensive. By using the basic principles of faux marble, but changing the colors, various fantasy marbles can be created which are a lot of fun when used in a less serious manner.

FANTASY MARBLE

SHOPPING LIST

MATERIALS

- Oil- or water-based black wall paint for the base coat
- Oil or acrylic scumble glaze
- Artists' oils or acrylics in black, white and pthalo green
- Gold powder
- Mineral spirits or denatured alcohol/methylated spirits

EQUIPMENT

- 1" (25 mm) decorators' brush
- Stippler brush
- Flat nylon brush
- Firm bristle brush
- Bob made out of T-shirt fabric
- Low-tack tape
- Sandpaper (440 grit)
- Natural sea sponge
- Gold auto tape for detail
- Protective latex gloves
- Plastic or canvas drop cloths to protect surfaces

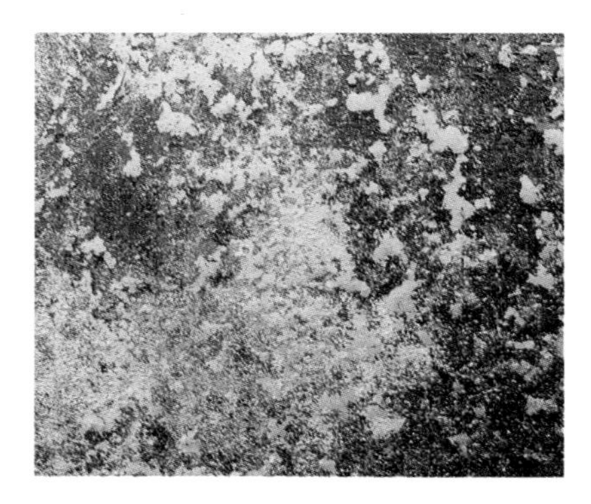

Fantasy marble does not resemble any particular marble but does carry some of the characteristics found in stone finishes. Fantasy finishes use a lot of basic marbling techniques and can be done in any number of colors that allow you to have fun and to experiment with paint without being bound by fixed rules. Being a bold finish, it is best not to use it for large areas, but it is effective on small boxes, picture frames, or as inlays on table tops.

1 Prepare the surface well and apply two base coats of black paint, sanding lightly between each coat to get a smooth surface.

2 Mix a black glaze using scumble glaze and artists' acrylic or oil pigments. Apply a thin layer of glaze to the surface and spread it evenly by painting back and forth a few times.

3 Wet a natural sea sponge in water and squeeze it out very well. Dip it into the gold powder and sponge onto the wet black glaze in heavily drifted patterns.

4 Spatter with the appropriate thinner for a solvent release effect (mineral spirits for oil-based glazes; denatured alcohol/methylated spirits for water-based glazes). Allow to dry completely.

5 Make a very thin glaze in whatever color you have chosen (our choice is pthalo green), and apply it thinly in random patches using a flat nylon brush.

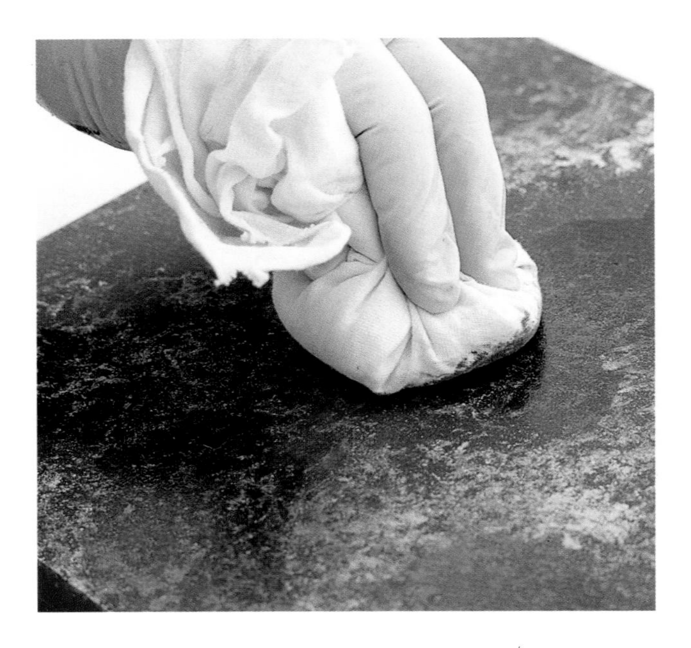

6 With a T-shirt bob lightly dab over the colored areas to soften the edges of the color.

7 Once again, spatter with mineral spirits (or denatured alcohol/methylated spirits if using water-based paint). Allow to dry.

8 When the fantasy marble finish has dried, you can either leave it as is or you can decorate the surface to make it more interesting. Here, gold auto tape has been used to create gold lines in the center of the lid.

9 To create a trompe l'oeil effect, mask off two opposite panels of the lid, mitering the corners. Mix a thin white glaze and a thin black glaze. Using a nylon brush, apply the white glaze to one panel and stipple to blend it, then repeat with the black glaze in the opposite panel. When both panels are dry, remove the tape and mask the other two panels. Apply thinner coats of the white and black glazes to create shadows and highlights. (See trompe l'oeil on p70.)

A fantasy marble jewelry box with a central pyramid stud that has been painted to look three dimensional.

TRAVERTINE

SHOPPING LIST

MATERIALS

- Oil- or water-based wall paint in pale beige tan for the base coat
- Artists' oils in raw sienna, burnt sienna, raw umber, white
- Oil-based scumble glaze
- Mineral spirits
- Matte varnish

EQUIPMENT

- 2" (50 mm) decorators' brush
- Japanese hake
- Round bristle brush
- Mounting board
- Craft knife
- Ruler
- Thick cardboard
- Paper towel
- Protective latex gloves
- Plastic or canvas drop cloths to protect surfaces

Travertine is a type of limestone that formed over long periods into horizontal compacted bands which range from cream to light gray and beige in color, and can be vibrant or quite subtle. Small openings, or pits, which are often created during the formation of travertine, can be quite challenging to recreate with paint. Because of its strong pattern, travertine is usually cut into tiles and laid down to create designs on floors or walls. If working directly onto a wall, divide it into tiles or panels and work each area separately. For a floor, have boards cut into equal sized 'tiles' and paint them individually (as shown here). Once painted and varnished, the wooden tiles can be glued to a cement floor (or a table top), leaving a small gap which can be lightly grouted using a gray tile grout.

1 Prepare the surface and apply two coats of the pale beige tan base color to give the look of natural travertine.

2 Mix four glazes to match the colors of natural travertine: pale cream, light caramel, pale burnt sienna and taupe (raw umber and white).

3 Apply different shades of glaze in wavy streaks diagonally across the board. The colors can overlap and blend into new colors. In some areas, make the bands of color different widths so that the pattern is irregular.

4 To remove excess paint and blend the colors, bunch a wad of paper towel and, with a shaking zigzag movement, pull it across the tile following the same direction as the wavy streaks.

5 Using a ruler and craft knife, cut a straight line across a 3" (8 cm) wide piece of thick cardboard. Only cut halfway through the cardboard and pull the two pieces apart, leaving a rough torn edge. For more distinct markings, cut some nicks in the edge of the cardboard.

6 In the same direction as before, following the bands of color, drag the cardboard through the glaze with the cut side on the top and the rough side underneath. As you pull the cardboard down, shake or quiver your hand so that the cardboard makes a distinct irregular track.

7 To achieve a solvent release effect, spatter some areas with clean mineral spirits to create small craters.

8 Lightly soften with a Japanese hake. This will slightly blur the lines without altering them.

9 Make a diluted mixture of raw umber and mineral spirits. Dip a bristle brush into this mixture and tap the brush gently on a stick or ruler to lightly spatter the surface. This will create the darker craters that also occur in travertine.

10 Travertine has a polished but semi-gloss finish so, when dry, use a matte varnish to protect the surface. If the tiles are to be used on a floor, apply three or four coats of varnish for extra protection.

Wooden tiles finished in faux travertine, and separated by white stones, transform an old cement floor.

FAUX EGYPTIAN GREEN MARBLE

SHOPPING LIST

MATERIALS

- Oil- or water-based wall paint in black for the base color
- Artists' oil or acrylic paint in terre verte (green earth)
- Artists' oil or eggshell enamel in titanium white, or white water-based acrylic or wall paint
- Artists' oil or acrylic scumble glaze
- Mineral spirits or denatured alcohol/methylated spirits
- Terebine driers
- High-gloss varnish

EQUIPMENT

- 2" (50 mm) decorators' brush or fine roller for base coat
- 3 or 4 feathers (large flight feathers)
- Fine artists' brush for veining
- Bristle brush for spattering
- Varnish brush
- Natural sea sponge
- Clean cloths or paper towel
- Protective latex gloves
- Plastic or canvas drop cloths to protect surfaces

Faux Egyptian green marble takes its inspiration from a number of dark green serpentine marbles, one of which, *verde antico* or antique green, has dark crystalline shapes; another, *Nefritica verde* is a type of jade. This theatrical faux finish is effective on large flat objects or surfaces, and on round or square columns, but it is not recommended for small items that would not normally be made of marble.

1 Prepare the surface and apply two coats of black paint for the base, sanding lightly between each coat. Mix a glaze using one-third scumble glaze, one third mineral spirits (or water for water-based paints) and one-third terre verte artists' color. If using oil-based paints, add a few drops of terebine driers.

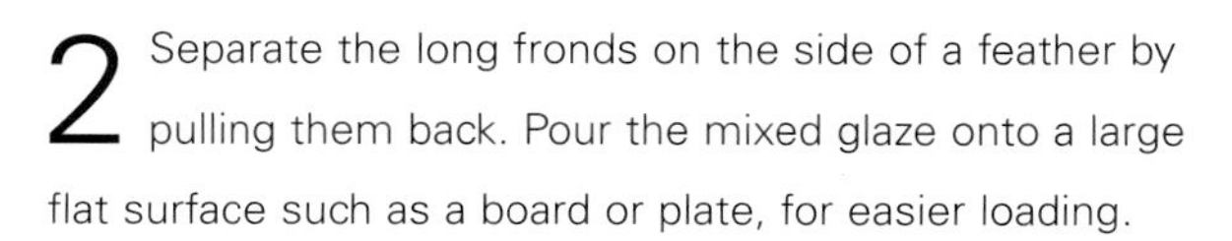

2 Separate the long fronds on the side of a feather by pulling them back. Pour the mixed glaze onto a large flat surface such as a board or plate, for easier loading.

3 Holding the feather in the middle of the shaft, drag it back and forth through the glaze to load it. Remove the excess by wiping the feather to and fro on a clean cloth or paper towel. Apply the glaze to the surface by pouncing and dabbing, constantly changing the direction of the feather. Try to create drifts of solid color.

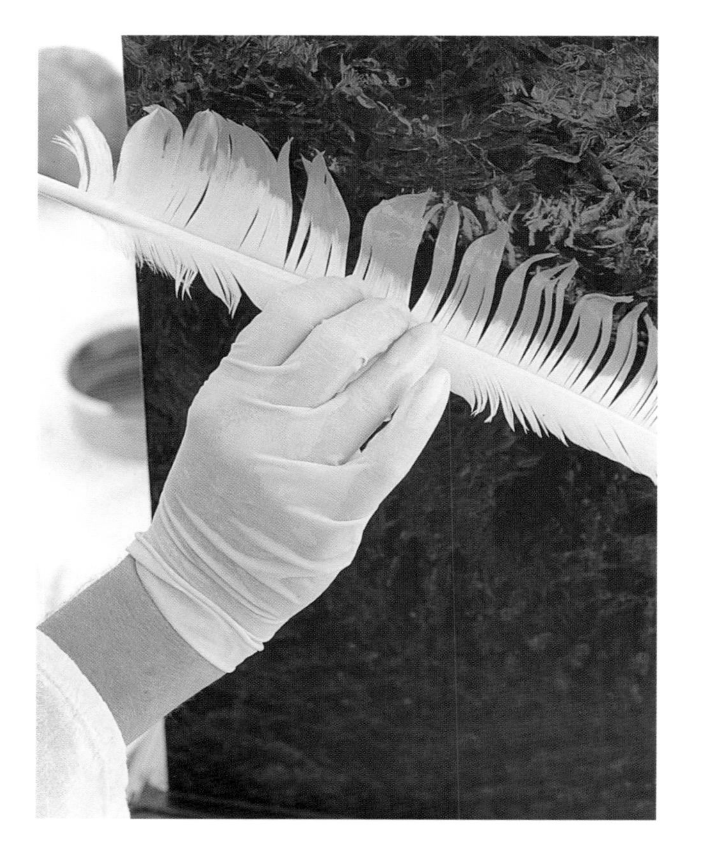

4 Dilute some titanium white paint with the appropriate thinner and add it to the green glaze to make it a shade lighter. Take a clean feather, prepared as before, and pounce the lighter color on top of the darker one. Randomly follow the drifts, leaving some black spaces, but do not make the second color as dense as the previous color.

5 Add more diluted white paint to the green glaze to make a third glaze that is even lighter. With another clean feather, pounce randomly as before, but sparingly, following some of the drifts.

6 Optional: While the glaze is still wet, use a stiff bristle brush to spatter the surface with the appropriate thinner for a solvent release effect. A sponge can be dipped in mineral spirits, squeezed out and dabbed onto some areas to achieve a similar effect.

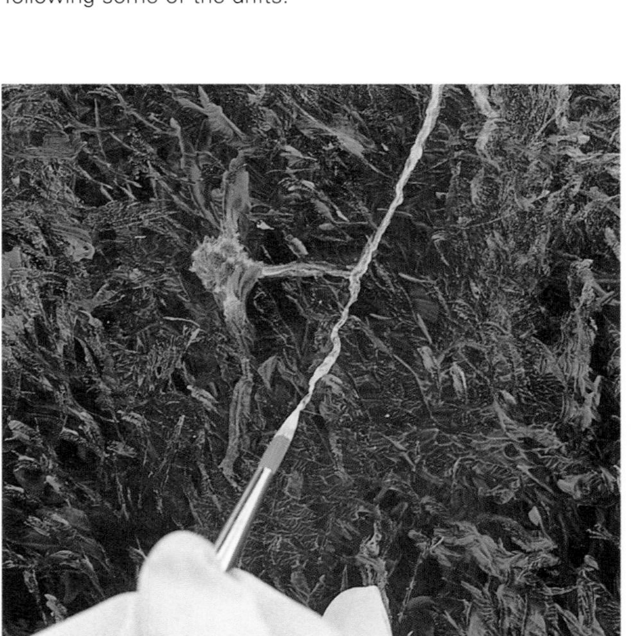

7 When dry, add a bit more white to the lightest glaze and, using a fine artists' brush, draw a few veins, joining up the drifts.

8 Apply two coats of high-gloss varnish to obtain a final polished stone effect.

Real marble is often carved into columns, so a painted faux marble column can look just like the real thing.

BLACK & WHITE MARBLE

SHOPPING LIST

MATERIALS

White oil-based wall paint for the base coat
Oil-based scumble glaze
Artists' oil paint in black
Mineral spirits
Terebine driers
High-gloss varnish

EQUIPMENT

Flat nylon brush
Fine artists' brush
Blotting paper sheets
Varnish brush
Protective latex gloves

This is one of the easiest faux marble finishes to do and the end result is bold and striking. It is particularly effective if done in large panels resembling cut slabs on a wall, such as in a bathroom; or in small tiles on the floor, as in travertine (see p100). It is not a specific marble, but is inspired by the many naturally occurring varieties of serpentine and grand antique marble.

1 Prepare the surface and paint with white oil-based paint.

2 Mix a strong black glaze using more black artists' oil paint than usual (see recipe on p18). Add a few drops of liquid driers to speed up the drying process.

3 Apply the glaze in an even, thin layer over the surface using a flat nylon artists' brush. When applying the glaze make sure your brush strokes slightly smooth out any marks left by the previous strokes.

4 Take a piece of blotting paper about 8" × 4" (20 × 10 cm) and scrunch it up along its length.

5 Holding it in both hands press it firmly into the black glaze at a slight diagonal angle. The blotting paper will pick up the glaze, leaving a fractured white mark. Repeat the action, turning the blotting paper to a clean side for each new mark. You will need to use clean blotting paper after two or three markings.

6 Dip a fine artists' brush into the mineral spirits and accentuate some of the white areas by removing more of the glaze and cleaning some of the larger markings. Join a few cracks and veins with very delicate lines. If any of the white areas become overworked and too white, delicately stipple over them with a small bristle brush.

7 Varnish with a high-gloss varnish.

A marbled wooden lamp base complements monotone design themes.

FAUX SIENA MARBLE

SHOPPING LIST

MATERIALS

Water-based:

- **Water-based white acrylic paint**
- **Acrylic scumble glaze**
- **Universal stainer or acrylic paint in raw umber, burnt umber, raw sienna, burnt sienna and white**
- **Denatured alcohol/methylated spirits**
- **Gloss acrylic varnish**
- **Water**

Oil-based:

- **Oil-based white wall paint**
- **Oil scumble glaze**
- **Artists' oils in raw umber, burnt umber, raw sienna, burnt sienna and white**
- **Mineral spirits**
- **Gloss oil varnish**

EQUIPMENT

- **Fine artists' brushes**
- **Flat nylon brush**
- **Small Japanese hake**
- **Round bristle brush**
- **Varnish brush**
- **Fine sandpaper (400 grit)**
- **Plastic wrap**
- **Bob made from T-shirt fabric**
- **Protective latex gloves**
- **Plastic or canvas drop cloths to protect surfaces**

Siena marble was the name given to stone originally quarried in and around the city of Siena in central Italy. Today it is used in reference to any predominantly yellow-colored marble. It can be recreated by using shades of raw sienna and burnt sienna glazes. ('Sienna' is the term for the yellow-brown colors made from ferric oxide pigment.) Faux Siena marble can be a strongly colored and veined stone. The technique is to build up layers of color and veining that are knocked back with softening and markings. Any faux marble can be created by this process, simply by changing the colors of the glazes.

1 Prepare the surface and apply two coats of white paint, sanding between coats to provide a smooth surface. Sand again with 400 grit paper to key the surface.

2 Mix each of the colors (raw umber, burnt umber, raw sienna and burnt sienna) with a little white to make four glazes. Further lighten the raw sienna with more white paint.

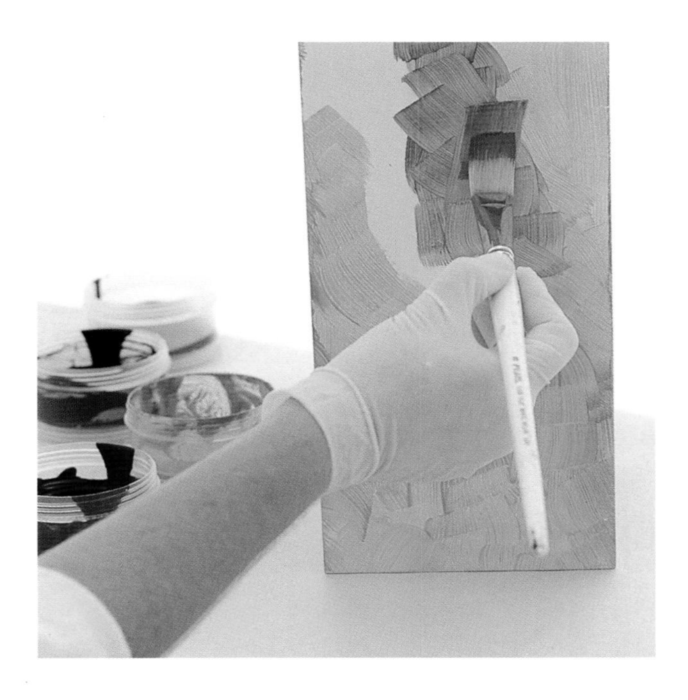

3 Using a flat nylon brush, apply the raw sienna and burnt sienna glazes in drifts covering the surface.

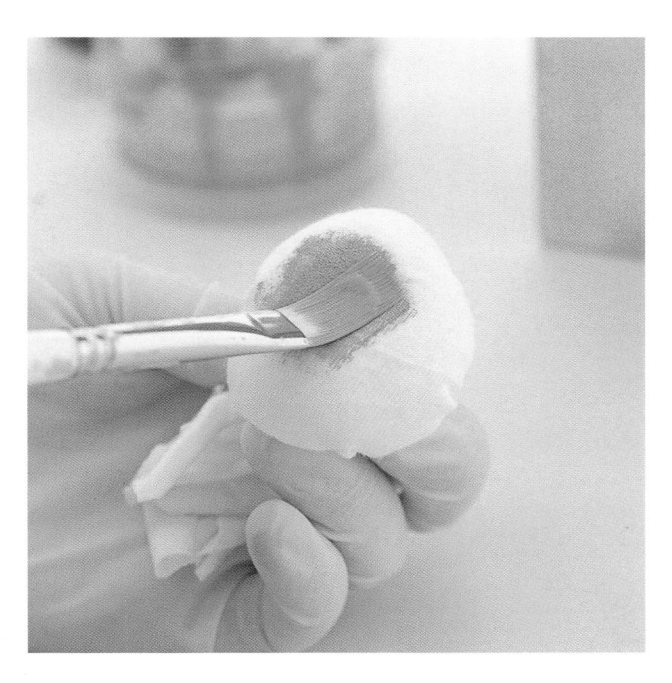

4 Make a small bob with soft T-shirt material. Start by buttering the bob with the raw sienna, then dab it over the raw sienna glaze to eliminate brush marks.

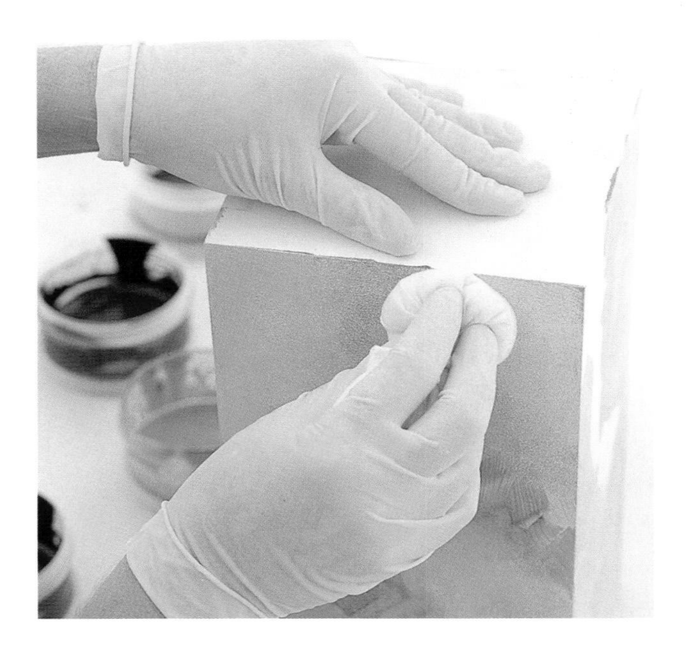

5 Next dab over the burnt sienna, slightly blending the two colors in the process. Wipe the bob clean at regular intervals as you work.

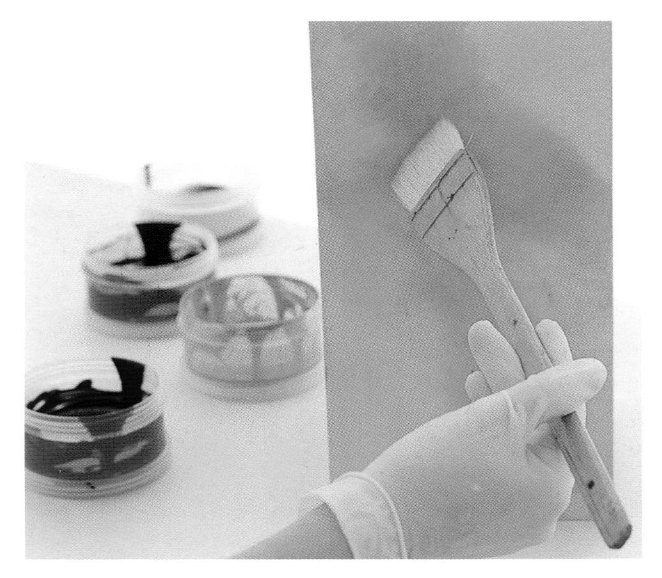

6 Soften the whole area with a small Japanese hake. A smaller brush is easier to control when working over the delicate markings of the marble.

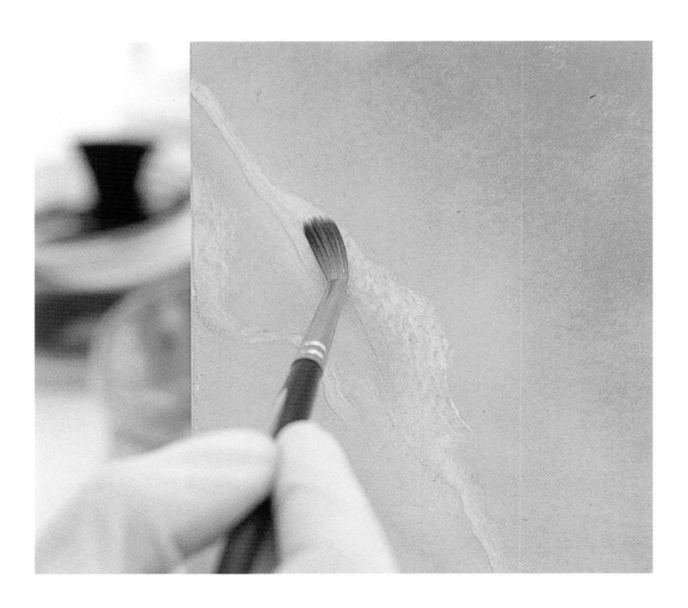

7 To create white veins with the solvent release method, dip a fine artists' brush into the appropriate thinner, then pull and roll the brush through the glaze, leaving some thin vein lines and larger 'cracks'.

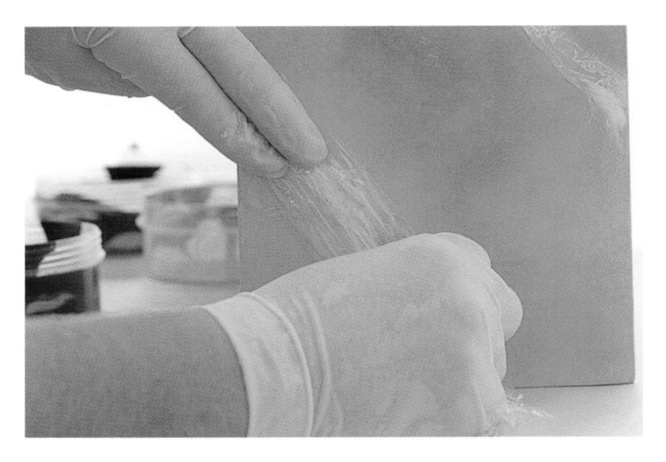

8 Using a piece of crinkled plastic wrap, press it along some of the cracks where glaze was removed with the solvent. This will leave a more fragmented white veining. Soften with the Japanese hake.

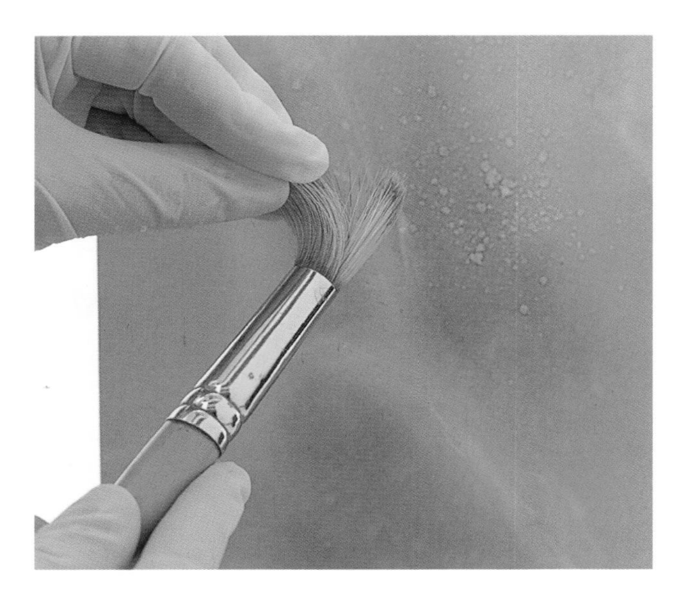

9 Dip a bristle brush into clean mineral spirits and, holding the brush above the surface, draw a finger through the bristles, spattering spirits over the area to create solvent release craters. Soften with the Japanese hake.

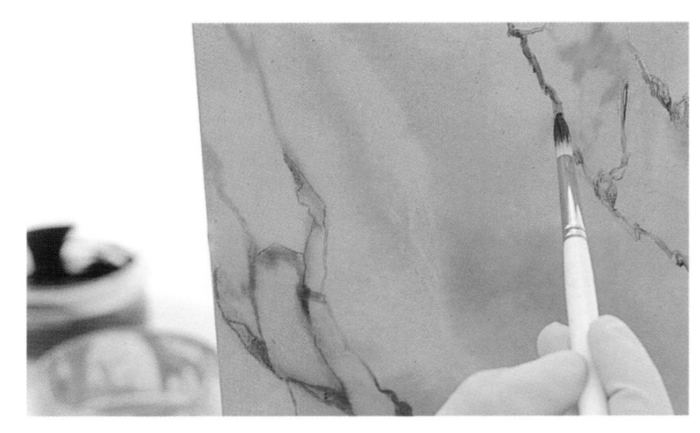

10 The final veins are dark lines that simulate cracks and fractures. They follow the markings previously made and, in some cases, even surround some of the lighter areas. Use a fine artists' brush and work with the raw and burnt umber glazes or burnt sienna. The number and color of veins you add at this stage is entirely optional. Some Siena marbles are densely crazed with dark veins, while some have very few. Soften the veins gently.

11 When dry, varnish with two coats of gloss varnish, as appropriate for the type of paint used.

A Siena marble lamp base complements the leather, wood and porcelain elements of this modern interior.

METAL LEAFING

Metal leafing, or gilding, is a technique used to recreate the traditional splendor of gold and silver objects and embellishments found in architecture. It can also be applied to a variety of functional items to create a contemporary look. By using either chemicals or paint, different dramatic effects can be obtained by tarnishing the gilding and changing its color. It works well on carved or molded objects and a number of surfaces are suitable for a metal leafing finish.

ALUMINUM LEAF

SHOPPING LIST

MATERIALS

- Oil-based wall paint in dark gray for the base coat
- Artists' oils in gray, ivory and black
- Oil-based gold size
- Aluminum transfer leaf
- Oil-based scumble glaze
- Terebine driers
- Mineral spirits

EQUIPMENT

- 2" (50 mm) flat brushes or fine roller for laying on base coat
- 1" (30 mm) flat brushes for applying size
- Firm bristle brush
- Japanese hake or other soft brush
- Stipple brush
- Scissors
- Silk bob or soft cloth
- Fine sandpaper (220 and 400 grit)
- Protective latex gloves
- Plastic or canvas drop cloths to protect surfaces

Aluminum is a good substitute for authentic silver leaf. It is less expensive and, as it does not tarnish, no varnish is required. It can be used effectively on furniture, picture frames and candlesticks and is ideal for outdoor use. It can be left in its shiny state, antiqued with glazes or sanded to give an old worn look.

Tip The 'open time' of gold size is the period during which you are able to stick the metal leaf to it before it dries completely.

1 It is important to ensure your surface is as smooth and even as possible. Once the object has been adequately primed, make sure that it is dust free, then paint it with the dark gray oil-based paint, ensuring all the molded indentations are well covered. Use a flat nylon brush to apply the base paint, spreading it out evenly to avoid brush marks. Apply two coats, sanding lightly with 220 grit paper between coats.

2 When dry, lightly sand the surface with 400 grit paper to remove all imperfections. Using a flat nylon brush and even brush strokes, cover the whole object with gold size. Avoid creating puddles of size in the molded areas. Leave for 12 hours, or the amount of time indicated on the size packaging (see tip on opposite page).

3 Touch the size with your knuckle to test when it is ready—it should feel tacky.

4 Cut the sheet of aluminum transfer leaf into usable sizes about 2" × 1½" (50 × 30 mm), as it is easier to press smaller pieces of leaf into the indentations.

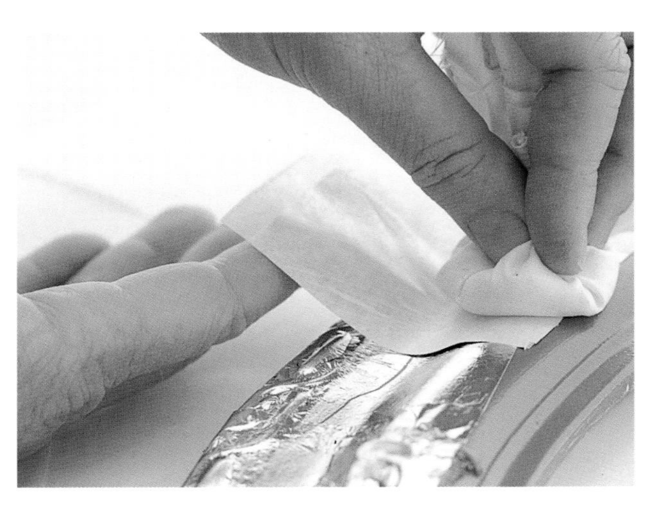

5 Take the transfer leaf to the object and, with the paper backing facing you, stick one edge of the metal leaf onto the surface. Then press down the whole piece with a silk bob or soft cloth. Lift off the backing paper.

6 Overlap the next piece slightly and continue until the entire object is covered. Use the silk bob to rub down the leaf quite firmly to smooth out the wrinkles. Allow at least 24 hours for the size to dry completely.

7 Take a soft paintbrush or Japanese hake and rub down the seams with short jabbing movements to remove the excess leaf and leave a clean join.

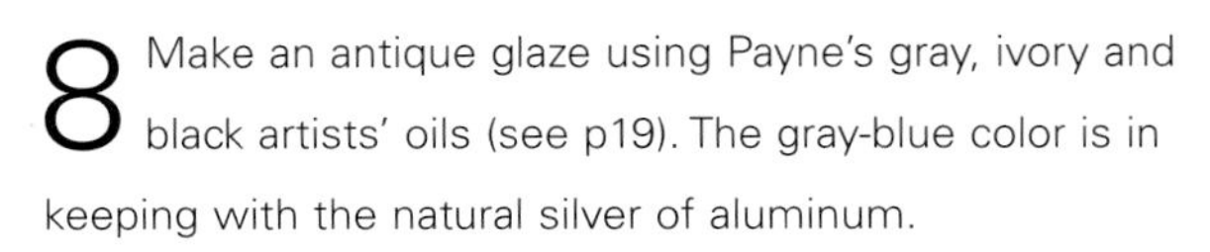

8 Make an antique glaze using Payne's gray, ivory and black artists' oils (see p19). The gray-blue color is in keeping with the natural silver of aluminum.

9 With a small firm bristle brush push the glaze into all the indentations of the molded areas. Do not use excessive amounts of glaze, as it will be too dark.

10 Stippling lifts excess glaze from the indentations and spreads it evenly, softening the color.

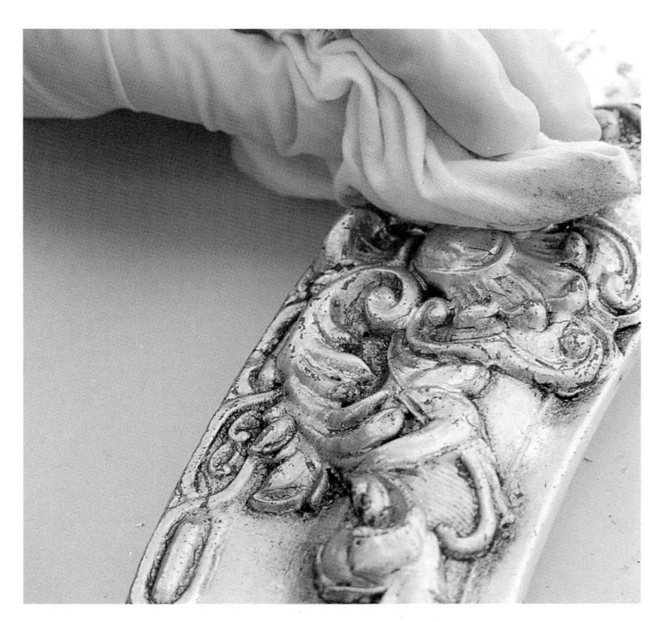

11 With a soft cloth, wipe clean all the raised areas of the molding.

Aluminum metal leaf has made a polyurethane plastic molded frame look like genuinely old silver.

COPPER & BRASS BURNING

SHOPPING LIST

MATERIALS

- Oil- or water-based wall paint in dark-red terracotta for base coat
- Brass transfer leaf (Dutch metal)
- Copper transfer leaf
- Gold size
- Cupric nitrate
- Ammonium chloride
- Barium sulphide
- Water
- Varnish

EQUIPMENT

- 1½" (30 mm) flat nylon brush
- Flat varnish brush
- Japanese hake
- Sandpaper (400 grit)
- Silk bob or soft cloth to rub metal leaf onto the size
- Cotton batting (upholsterers' cotton)
- Small jars, measuring spoons and measuring cup
- Protective latex gloves
- Protective face mask
- Plastic or canvas drop cloths to protect surfaces

Tip Small quantities of chemicals such as cupric nitrate, ammonium chloride and barium sulphide can be obtained from a pharmacy.

The natural tarnishing that occurs on metal objects can be successfully imitated by applying the correct paint and antiquing glazes to metal leaf. The following techniques illustrate how to distress metal leaf by applying chemicals which activate the tarnishing process. Although the chemicals used are mild and not harmful, it is advisable to wear a face mask, and latex gloves to protect your hands.

SURFACE PREPARATION

1 Prepare the surface and paint it with two coats of dark red terracotta paint for the base. The final surface must be very smooth, so sand between each coat with 400 grit paper.

The following five steps are the same for applying both brass and copper leaf.

2 With a flat nylon brush, cover the whole object with gold size, using even brush strokes. Avoid leaving puddles of size in the molded areas. Leave for 12 hours, or the amount of time indicated on the size packaging (see p116).

3 Cut the sheet of transfer leaf into usable sizes as it is easier to handle smaller pieces of metal leaf.

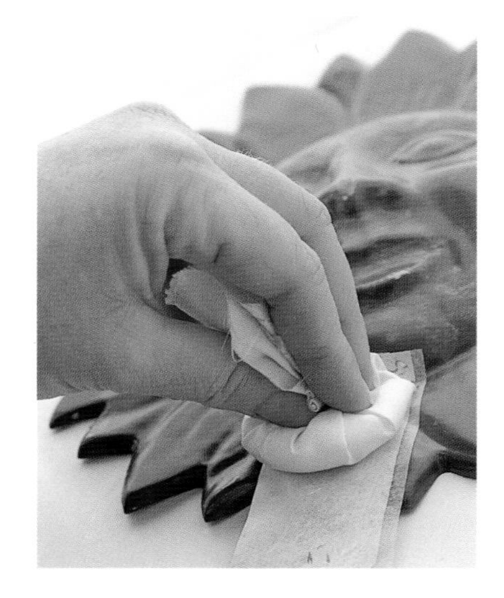

4 Take the leaf to the object and, with the paper backing facing you, stick one edge of the metal leaf onto the surface. Then dab down the whole piece with a bob or soft cloth. Lift off the backing paper.

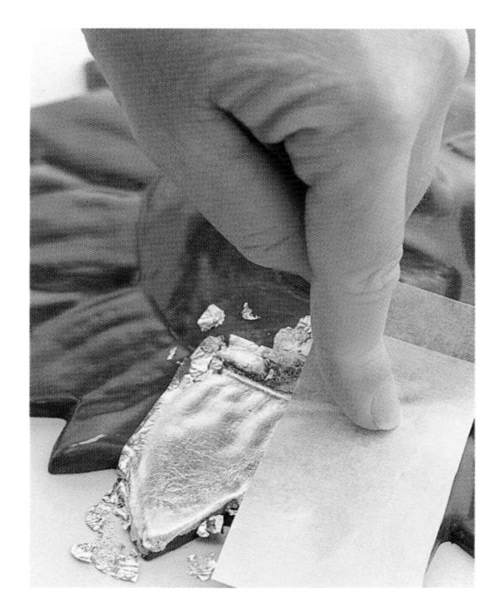

5 Overlap the next piece slightly and continue in this way until the entire object is covered. Use a silk bob to rub down the leaf quite firmly to smooth out the wrinkles. Allow at least 24 hours for the size to dry.

6 Take a soft paintbrush, such as a Japanese hake, and rub down the seams with short jabbing movements to remove the excess leaf and leave a clean join.

COPPER LEAF WITH BARIUM SULPHIDE

1 Mix the chemical formula by dissolving ¼ teaspoon of barium sulphide in half a cup of warm water. The barium sulphide does not dissolve completely so you must stir it each time you want to apply it.

2 Using cotton batting, apply the chemical mixture to the leafed surface, allowing it to puddle in the hollows. The chemical will ciss (form small pools) so you must constantly work over the surface with the batting until you have enough of the area covered.

3 Leave the chemical mixture on for about 30 minutes, or until the tarnishing is to your requirements. If you leave it overnight, it will go completely black.

4 Rinse the chemical off with water and dab dry. Finish by varnishing.

BRASS LEAF WITH CUPRIC NITRATE

1 Mix the chemical formula by dissolving ½ teaspoon of cupric nitrate in ½ teaspoon of warm water. Separately dissolve ½ teaspoon ammonium chloride in two teaspoons of warm water. Mix both together and add one cup of warm water for a full-strength mixture.

2 Apply the chemical mixture to the leafed surface using cotton batting (upholsterers' cotton), allowing it to puddle in the hollows. The chemical will ciss on the surface so you must constantly work over the surface with the batting until you have enough of the area covered.

3 Leave the chemical on the surface until you notice that the metal leaf has started to tarnish to a vivid green color.

4 Neutralize the process by placing a wet cloth over the whole surface. Wash the chemicals off with water and pat dry.

Note: do not varnish, as this will remove the green color.

Chemical tarnishing makes these gilded suns look as if they are made from metal that has weathered naturally.

METALLIC & PEARLESCENT POWDERS

SHOPPING LIST

MATERIALS

Pearl luster powders in platinum gold (for the leaves) and a rich pale gold (for the spaces between the leaves and for the leaf veins)

Water-based gold size or varnish (the advantage of gold size is that it has a longer 'open time')

EQUIPMENT

Flat nylon brush

Japanese hake or soft dusting brush for powders

Assortment of artists' fitches

2B pencil

Large sheets of paper (at least 12" × 12"/30 × 30 cm in size)

Tracing paper

Graphite paper

Scissors or craft knife

Face mask (to avoid inhaling metallic powders)

Artists' fixative or hair spray

Protective latex gloves

Plastic or canvas drop cloths to protect surfaces

Pearlescent powders and paints create a glowing, lustrous effect that is reminiscent of the mother of pearl in sea shells. They gather and reflect light, giving a soft and elegant impression. Silvery pearl glazes and powders come in breathtaking colors, from the palest pastels to the richest golds. When applied over different base coats, the colors change subtly and vary according to changing light conditions. They are especially effective when highlighting rounded surfaces like vases, columns, accessories and architectural features. We have chosen a leaf design, inspired by beautiful wallpaper, which can be applied to a table top, tray, box or ornament. If you are working on a wall, you will have to use a stencil to apply the design.

1 Find some references for big leaves by either collecting real leaves or making photocopies from books. Draw or trace several leaves onto sheets of paper, then cut each one out.

2 After cutting out the leaves, position them on a large sheet of paper. The gaps between the leaves should be roughly the same size. Draw around the outline of the leaves on the paper.

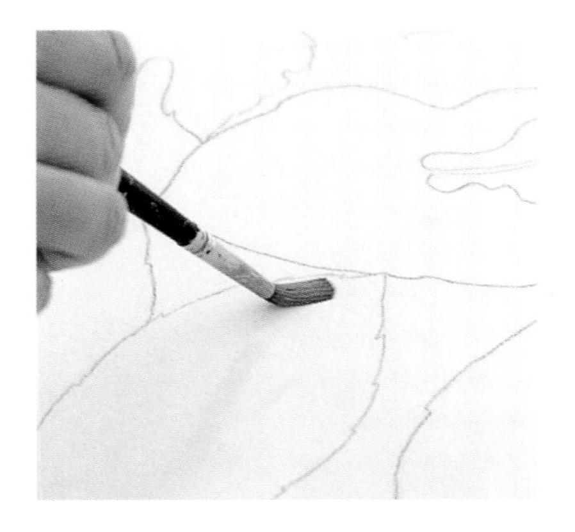

3 When you have transferred the design to the surface, paint the leaves with water-based gold size. (If this is unobtainable, use a clear varnish instead.)

4 When the size is tack dry, wear a mask, then dip a brush into the platinum gold powder and dust it onto the tacky size, brushing it to and fro. Shake off excess powder.

5 When each leaf is completely dry, use water-based gold size to paint the areas between the leaves that are to be gold. Dust the powder onto these areas (as in step 4).

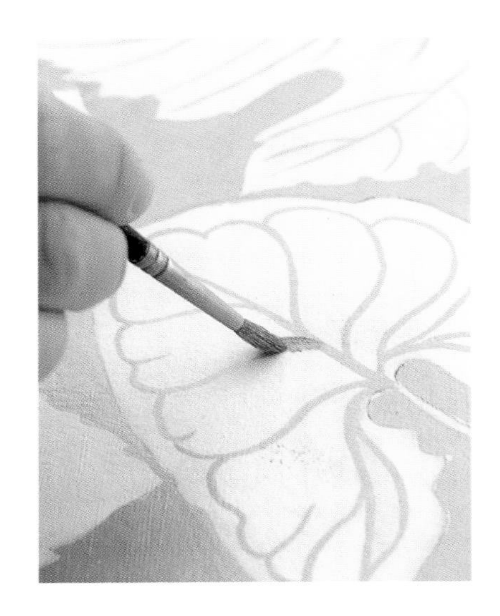

6 Use a small artists' fitch and water-based gold size to paint in the veins of the leaves. When these are tack dry, dust with gold powder and remove excess.

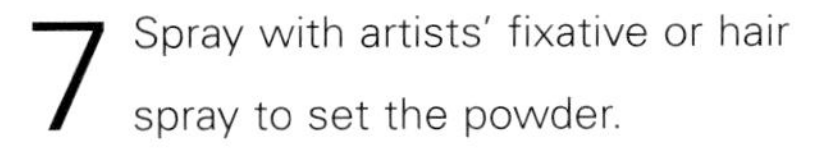

7 Spray with artists' fixative or hair spray to set the powder.

This beautiful wallpaper inspired the design illustrated in this project.

GLOSSARY

Acrylic	Water-based paint that becomes waterproof when dry.
Antiquing	Processes used to simulate natural ageing, wear and tear.
Balustrade	A row of shapely balusters or posts topped with a handrail.
Bob	A ball of upholsterer's cotton wrapped in a square of silk or T-shirt fabric and secured with a rubber band. Used to polish or smooth off fine paint surfaces.
Cissing	The effect created when solvent is spattered onto a painted surface that is still wet.
Decoupage	The art of cutting out pictures and applying them to a surface.
Dragging	Technique for pulling a long-haired brush through wet paint or glaze to produce a series of fine lines.
Faux	A French term meaning fake or imitation.
Glaze	Transparent or semi-transparent medium (oil- or water-based).
Grisaille	Painting in gray monotone, usually in trompe l'oeil representations of architectural details.
Grout	Thin mortar used to fill joints between tiles.
Heart grain	The grain pattern on wood, obtained by cutting through the length of the tree and revealing the annular growth rings. (Also known as heart wood.)
Marbling	Variety of paint techniques designed to recreate artificially the appearance of marble.
Medullary rays	Rays of sap which radiate out from the center of the tree. Quartered wood, such as oak, displays this as silver grain or dapples.
Moiré	Watermarked silk or taffeta.
Mural	A painting done directly onto a wall.
Mutton cloth	Soft, cotton, stockinette fabric, usually knitted in a tube
Plumb line	A length of string with a weight tied to the bottom, used to obtain straight vertical lines down walls.
Polyurethane	Synthetic resin used on some paints and varnish.
Ragging	A technique that uses a crumpled rag to create decorative broken color finishes.
Size	An adhesive varnish with a drying (open) time of between one and 12 hours, used to hold down metal leaf.
Spattering	A painting technique in which a brush dipped in paint, glaze or varnish is knocked to spray dots of color onto a surface.
Sponging	A painting technique that uses a damp sponge to create a mottled patchy effect.
Stippling	A technique used to soften and blend color, and eliminate brush strokes.
Terebine driers	A blend of lead, calcium and cobalt driers.
Thixotropic	A term used to describe paint that returns to a gel state after mixing.
Trellis	A structure of flat strips of wood or metal crossing each other, used decoratively against a wall. (Also known as lattice.)
Trompe l'oeil	Painting which creates an optical illusion or 'deceives the eye'.
TSP	Trisodium phosphate, used for cleaning and stripping paint.

SUPPLIERS

Art Supply Stores
(specialty paints and mediums, artists' paintbrushes and tools, leafing supplies)

Craft Supply Stores
(artists' paintbrushes and tools, artists' oil paints and mediums, acrylic paints and mediums, leafing supplies)

Home Improvement Centers
(paints, primers, sealers, paintbrushes, general paint supplies)

The Art Store
(nationwide locations)
www.artstores.com
(artists' oils, acrylic paints and tools)

Johnson Paint Company
355 Newbury Street
Boston, MA 02115
Tel: (617) 536-4244
www.johnsonpaint.com
(comprehensive collection of fine quality painting tools and supplies for faux finishing, including specialty paints, glazes, varnishes, and gilding supplies)

Michaels Stores
(nationwide locations)
www.michaels.com
(artists' oils, acrylic paints and tools, gilding supplies)

Pearl Paint
308 Canal Street
New York, NY 10013
Tel: (800) 221-6845
www.pearlpaint.com
(artists' oils, acrylic paints and tools, gilding supplies)

Spectra Paint
7615 Balboa Boulevard
Van Nuys, CA 91406
Tel: (818) 786-5610
www.spectrapaint.com
(comprehensive collection of fine quality painting tools and supplies for faux finishing, including specialty paints, glazes and varnishes)

Winsor & Newton
P.O. Box 1396
Piscataway, NJ 08855
www.winsornewton.com
(specialty paints and mediums, artists' paintbrushes and tools)

CREDITS AND ACKNOWLEDGEMENTS

All photographs by Warren Heath except: Deidi von Schaewen: cover (bottom right), pp1, 2–3, 4, 5, 7, 8, 9, 28, 34, 35, 36, 37, 48, 65 (bottom right), 77, 78, 83, 94, 95, 114, 115, 125 (bottom right); Craig Fraser: p27; Louise Hennigs: pp56, 57, 89.

The authors and publisher wish to thank the following: Mavromac, suppliers of Loumac fabric; Le Papier du Port, for artists' brushes and equipment; and World of Interiors, all of Cape Town. Claudia Derain and Hari Ajwani of the Nilaya Hermitage Hotel, Goa, India. The owners, architects and designers of the featured homes: Marie Beltrami, Cecile & Boyd's, Ramuntcho de Saint Armand, Brigitte Lecetre, Philippe Model, Pierre Peyrol, Ann and Patrick Poirer, Jeff Sayre, Kathrine Warren and Lillian Williams. The mural on p57 and the entire room featured on p89 were painted by Louise Hennigs.

INDEX